A SHELTER IS NOT A HOME...
OR IS IT?

A Shelter Is Not A Home...
Or Is It?

*Lessons from Family Homelessness in
New York City*

Ralph da Costa Nunez

President of Homes for the Homeless

Foreword by
Leonard N. Stern

Founder of Homes for the Homeless

WHITE TIGER PRESS • NEW YORK

Library of Congress Cataloging-in-Publication Data

Cover photography and design: © James E. Farnum

ISBN 0-9724425-0-2

© 2004 Homes for the Homeless, Inc.
White Tiger Press
521 West 49th Street, New York, NY 10019

A White Tiger Book

Printed in the United States of America

Dedicated to the memory of Senator Daniel Patrick Moynihan, who understood poverty better than any of us.

CONTENTS

Foreword by *Leonard N. Stern*   xvii

Preface   xxi

Acknowledgements   xxiii

Introduction   1

    Homelessness in New York City: An Overview
    A New Poverty: The New Homeless

1. The Early 1980s
    A First Response to a Growing Crisis   7

    The Economy
    Social Service Cuts
    Lack of Affordable Housing
    Contributing Factors
    The Emergency Shelter Build-Up
    Responses from the Public and the Courts

2. The Mid 1980s
    Emergency Efforts: The EAU and Welfare Hotels   19

    Emergency Assistance Units
    Tier I Facilities
    Welfare Hotels
    Hotel Scrutiny: The Media's Role
    From Emergency Responses to Long-Term Solutions
    The Move Towards Transitional Housing

3. The Late 1980s and Early 1990s
   Old Problems, New Strategies   29

   A New Agency
   Transitioning to Tier II
   Local Resistance: Not In My Back Yard
   Steps Forward, Steps Back
   Emergency Assistance: The Federal Approach
   New Directions: Tightening the Door

4. The Mid 1990s
   Getting Tough: A New Administration's Approach   43

   National Context
   City Welfare Reforms
   The New Homeless Journey
   Attacks on Low-Income Housing
   More Controversy
   Reflections

5. The Late 1990s and Beyond
   Conflict and Consensus   55

   Change for the Better
   Shelters: Yesterday and Today
      The Long Journey
      Something Old Is Something New

6. Coming Home
   The Reality of Housing Policy   65

   Losing the Battle: The Declining Housing Stock
   New York City: Unique Challenges
   Possible Solutions: Proposals from Advocates
      Rental Subsidies

Supportive Housing
A New Dialogue: From Housing to Shelters

7. A Poverty of Adults: Homeless Parents Today   75

Domestic Violence
Foster Care
Teenage Pregnancy
Job Readiness
Welfare Reform
What Can Be Done

8. A Poverty of Youth: Homeless Children Today   91

Education
Enrollment, Transfers, and Absences
The Youngest Learners
Unprepared Parents
Children's Health
Homeless and Hungry
Emotional Well-Being
Putting It Together: Health and School Performance
What Can Be Done and Where Can We Do It?

9. New Communities of Opportunity   103

Shelters and Learning
Shelters and Employment
Shelters and Foster Care
Shelters and Teen Pregnancy
Shelters and Domestic Violence
Shelters and Children's Health
Shelters and Community

Bibliography	**117**
Index	**131**

FIGURES AND TABLES

FIGURES

1.1: Average Daily Family Shelter Census: New York City (1982 to 1988) — 8

1.2: Renter Households with Incomes Below the Poverty Level by New York City Borough (1983) — 9

1.3: The Percent Change in Federal Spending: Social vs. Military Programs (1980 to 1990) — 10

1.4: Decrease in HUD Budget Spending for Housing Assistance (1981 to 1989) — 11

2.1: Percent of Families Placed by Type of Shelter: New York City (1986) — 21

2.2: Number of Families Residing in Commercial Welfare Hotels: New York City (1984 to 1986) — 23

3.1: Average Daily Family Shelter Census: New York City (1987 to 1993) — 29

3.2: Average Number of Families Seen Per Night at the EAU: New York City (1987 to 1993) — 29

3.3: Distribution of Families in Temporary Housing: New York City (1987 to 1992) — 30

3.4: Number of Tier II Family Centers: New York City
(1984 to 1988)   34

3.5: One Time EARP Bonus by Number of Family
Members   35

3.6: Distribution of Families Relocated to Permanent
Housing: New York City (1990 and 1993)   36

3.7: Allocation of McKinney Act Funding by Percent
(1993)   38

4.1: Homeless Families Denied Shelter: New York City
(1995 and 1998)   47

4.2: City Owned Vacant and Occupied Housing Units:
New York City (1994 to 2002)   48

4.3: Building Blocks Program: Housing Units Returned to
Private Sector in New York City (1996 to 2002)   49

5.1: Average Daily Family Shelter Census: New York City
(1982 to 2003)   55

5.2: Average Number of Overnight Stays at the New York
City Emergency Assistance Unit (1998 to 2003)   56

6.1: Length of Wait for Section 8 in Selected Cities (1999) 66

6.2: Decline in Vacant Available Low-Income Housing
Units by Rent: New York City (1996 to 1999)   68

7.1: Racial Profile of New York City Families:
All Families vs. Homeless Families   76

7.2: Homeless Parents Who Experienced Domestic
Violence   77

7.3: Homeless Parents Who Entered Shelters as a Result of
Domestic Violence   77

7.4: Homeless Parents with a Foster Care History   79

7.5: Number of Children in Foster Care vs. the Number of
Children in Shelters: New York City (1998 to 2003)   80

7.6: Age When Homeless Women Became Pregnant
with Their First Child   81

7.7: Age at Which Homeless Teen Mothers First Had Sex:
New York City   81

7.8: Birth Control Knowledge Among Homeless Teenage
Mothers: New York City   82

7.9: Decline in Welfare Rolls: New York City Recipients
(1995 to 2003)   85

8.1: Educational Setbacks Among Homeless Children:
New York City   91

8.2: Homeless Children School Transfers in a Single Year:
New York City   92

8.3: School Travel Times for Homeless Children:
New York City (2002)   93

8.4: Schools Attended by Homeless Children Living at the
Saratoga Family Inn: New York City (2002)   94

8.5: Developmental Delays and Preschool Enrollment of
Homeless vs. Non-Homeless Children   95

8.6: Impact of Food Intake on Homeless Children's
Health   98

8.7: Hunger: Homeless vs. Non-Homeless Children   98

8.8: Emotional Well-Being of Homeless Children:
New York City vs. National   98

9.1: Homeless Children Enrolled in After-School Programs:
Grade Improvement by Academic Subject   107

TABLES

1.1: Available Vacant Units by Monthly Contract Rent:
New York City (1984 and 1987)   12

6.1: New York City Housing Characteristics   67

7.1: Homeless Parent Profile: New York City
(1987 and 2002)   75

7.2: Comparison of Homeless Parents: With and Without
a Foster Care History   79

7.3: Characteristics of Women Receiving Public Assistance
and in Job Training Programs in New York City:
Non-Homeless vs. Homeless   84

7.4: The Qualifications Needed for Public Assistance
Recipients to Participate in a Typical Job Training
Program vs. the Typical Female Homeless
Head-of-Household   84

7.5: Public Assistance Applications and Rejections:
New York City (1993 to 2002)   86

8.1: Health Problems Among Homeless Children:
New York City   97

FOREWORD

The story of homelessness for me is a journey that began almost two decades ago when Edward Koch was New York City Mayor and I first visited the Roberto Clemente family shelter in the Bronx. Until that time I had no idea what homelessness really was. Like most New Yorkers, I thought the homeless were grown men, and in some cases women, who either had a mental illness, had a substance abuse problem, or were simply down on their luck. You could see them on street corners, on benches in parks, or sleeping in doorways, and you would almost always try to avoid them.

But on that evening in the autumn of 1985, when I walked into the Clemente shelter, I was stunned. I could not believe that entire families with children were also homeless. I would soon learn that they are the fastest growing segment of the homeless population, and at Clemente it was obvious. The facility was a large open gymnasium that had been converted into a makeshift congregate shelter. There were hundreds of cots pushed together on an open floor, congregate bathrooms, and fluorescent lights that stayed on all night long. Everywhere you looked there were state troopers standing guard, and there was nothing about the place that would make anyone feel safe or glad to be there.

It was then that I decided that something more needed to be done, and the public at large needed to know that homelessness was also about children. With the help of Mayor Koch and his administration, along with Reverend James Parks Morton of the Cathedral of St. John the Divine, I established Homes for the

Homeless, a not-for-profit organization that would immediately begin providing clean, safe, and humane transitional housing for homeless families with children until they secured a permanent housing placement.

In 1986 we opened our first facility, the Prospect Family Inn, formerly a private proprietary hospital in the Bronx. Over the next few months, we would open two more Inns—the Saratoga Family Inn in Queens and the Island Family Inn in Staten Island. In less than a year's time, we would be housing twice the number of families I saw at the Clemente shelter and twelve percent (12%) of the city's overall family shelter population. But as time went on, I began to understand that homelessness was about something more than just housing. It was a symptom of a severe, debilitating poverty. The families who came to our Inns were not just there because they needed a place to live; they had all kinds of social needs.

Over the last seventeen years I have met women who were the victims of domestic violence; people who wanted to go to work, but just did not have the skills; and very young mothers, with young children, caught up in the calamity of events—not understanding how they got there and not knowing where they were going next. But if anything has moved me and provided a challenge to do something about the scourge of homelessness, it is the children. Although homelessness affects people of all ages, it is the children who are the real victims. They have done nothing to deserve this, yet their numbers and suffering continue to grow. Today, there are many more children in New York City shelters than there are adults, so that the typical homeless person in the city is now a young child.

In a nation that prides itself on the state and well-being of its children, we as a society need to ensure that homeless children have a future, a chance to learn, play, and experience childhood. Nothing is more disheartening than to hear a child say, "When I grow up, I'm going to be a teacher, a fireman, a nurse, or a lawyer," and to know that their hopes and dreams may never come true without support to help them and their families. That support has been the mission of Homes for the Homeless.

When my journey into the world of homelessness began, I never imagined that it would go on for so long. Four mayors have come and gone, each grappling with this issue in their own way. Some built more shelters; others closed them. There have been many new initiatives and requirements, but the homeless kept coming. In the seventeen years since Homes for the Homeless first opened its doors, we have served over 22,000 families with 41,000 children in our facilities, helping them move on to more productive lives, and we continue to expand our mission. Not everyone needed all the services we provided, but everyone benefited from something. Like the young girl in a family of five at the Saratoga Family Inn. Only she and her mother were living together; her three siblings were all in alternative care. Her mother went through our job training program and eventually got a job. The girl excelled in our accelerated after-school programs, and was accepted into the Bronx School of Science, one of New York's most competitive and elite high schools. She and her mother were able to move into permanent housing, and they brought the whole family back together. Today, this girl is a junior at Bryn Mawr College, one of the nation's top women's colleges. Empowered by her own experience, last summer she returned to work with other homeless children at Homes for the Homeless' sleep-away camps.

That is why homelessness truly is the story of families in need of assistance and children who need to be ensured of an education. And that is why in 1993 and 1999 Homes for the Homeless opened its Clinton and Springfield Family Inns and plans to open two more Inns in the near future. In the end, we will eventually house almost eight hundred families a night. We will continue to operate our summer camps in Harriman State Park and send over one-thousand children there each summer. Our Institute for Children and Poverty will continue to do research, collect data, and publish articles, reports, and books, so that one of the most inextricable and misunderstood issues of our time can be dealt with in meaningful ways.

We have come a long way with this issue, but until every homeless boy, girl, and parent stands on equal ground with equal opportunities to participate in the American Dream, our work is not done. This new book, while telling the story of family homelessness in New York City, a story of which so many of us are a part, also provides a blueprint for the future—a new way to look at homelessness, and a new way to begin to bring about its end. It is my hope that the day will come when no child or family is homeless in America, and shelters are a thing of the past.

January 2004   Leonard N. Stern
New York City

PREFACE

A Shelter Is Not a Home...Or Is It? is the product of over 20 years of working with homeless families. During that period, there have been numerous plans to reduce homelessness and theories to explain its causes– first and foremost the lack of affordable housing. But family homelessness persists, and is worse today than at any time before. Each evening across America hundreds of thousands of men, women, and children sleep in abandoned buildings, tents, shelters, or on the streets – they are homeless. Hundreds of thousands more live doubled and tripled up in tenuous housing situations – sometime in the future they will be homeless as well.

Will it ever end? Simply looking at the obstacles these families face: histories of foster care and domestic violence, a lack of employment options and affordable housing, and multiple episodes of homelessness, the picture is bleak. And with their children transferring schools multiple times, getting left back and placed into special education, dropping out all together as adolescents, and being taunted and chastised simply because they have no place to call home, it is worse. But *A Shelter Is Not a Home* is their story. It traces the evolution of family homelessness in New York City, the homeless capital of America. It also measures government responses to this crisis and looks at research findings surrounding its root causes.

Today, more than ever before, family homelessness appears to be a permanent part of the poverty landscape, and experience seems to demonstrate that housing alone will not solve the problem. If we are ever going to truly begin to end family homelessness, we must understand that it encompasses a multitude of social ills. We also have to come to grips with the fact that little low-income housing has been built and even less appears to be on the horizon. And we must begin to deal with family homelessness where we have the greatest ability to have the broadest impact; in shelters where these families currently reside. This book is a first step in that process, and NYC is the case study that holds the answer to reducing family homelessness once and for all.

January 2004   Ralph da Costa Nunez
New York City

ACKNOWLEDGEMENTS

A Shelter Is Not a Home...Or Is It? is the product of years of observation, discussion, and research concerning the issue of family homelessness. Without the input of former city officials and the hard work of the staff at the Institute for Children and Poverty it could never have been done. In particular, I would like to thank Nancy Wackstein, Ken Murphy, and Larry Schatt, former city officials for providing us with so much government insight. Sal Tuchelli, former operator of the Martinique Hotel, for sharing his point of view and experiences working with homeless families. At the Institute for Children and Poverty, Elizabeth Clarke, Jesse Ellison, Erin Thompson, and Amanda Glatzel spent hours upon hours researching and organizing so many aspects of this work. And then there is Laura Caruso and Karina Kwok, and all the others who were willing to read various sections of the manuscript and comment on many of the ideas that emerged in the text; I am grateful to all of them as well. In the end, *A Shelter Is Not a Home* is really the product of an extremely supportive board of directors at Homes for the Homeless and the Institute. They have always challenged us to explore the root causes of family homelessness and push the envelope in seeking common-sense solutions.

INTRODUCTION

New York City has always been a beacon for those in search of prosperity, and the success of those who helped shape it into one of the world's premier cultural and financial capitals is well known. But hidden are the stories of the many that found poverty instead of wealth. Rich and poor have long coexisted in New York, and nowhere in America are class disparities so glaring. Yet today, there is a new kind of poverty, an epidemic of destitution that is largely hidden from public view. Family homelessness has grown exponentially in the last two decades, and its victims are the city's most vulnerable citizens: young single women and their children.

Children now make up nearly half (44%) of the total shelter population in New York City, and for an entire generation, a shelter may be their only home.[1] But how did this happen? How in the city of dreams could such a nightmare take place? Homelessness remains one of the most misunderstood issues of our time. It is not simply a story of housing needs, but rather part of a larger picture in which social ills and economic instability have created a new poverty in America.

This book tells the story of family homelessness in New York City, how it first emerged in the 1980s and quickly became entrenched in the urban landscape. It answers the questions: Who are today's homeless families? Where do they come from? What challenges do they face? What does their future hold? And how has the government responded to homelessness and why have these responses often exacerbated the problem?

When I first began to work with homelessness in the early eighties, in the office of then Mayor Koch, neither I, nor anyone else involved, ever thought that it would continue for the next twenty years, or that it would get worse. But it has, and there is still a critical need for new thinking and new insight. By looking back and understanding family homelessness in its entirety—as an all-encompassing poverty—we have a chance to develop new policies that make sense and make a difference. Understanding homelessness as a chronic and perhaps permanent problem in America helps us begin to address its root causes more comprehensively, and hopefully, help prevent more children from becoming trapped in a cycle that has already claimed so many.

HOMELESSNESS IN NEW YORK CITY: AN OVERVIEW

Homelessness is not a new problem for New York. At the turn of the 20th century, city leaders were already grappling with a fifty percent poverty rate. Urbanization and immigration led to an acute overcrowding in city housing. In the city's poorest neighborhoods, such as the Bowery, the destitute found a night's rest on a hammock in a flophouse or inside a five by seven foot sleeping cage at a cage hotel. And these were not just adults, beginning as early as the mid-1800s, there were an estimated thirty-thousand homeless children on New York's streets.[2]

Jacob Riis' seminal 1890 work, "How the Other Half Lives: Studies Among the Tenements of New York," exposed squalid tenement housing and the plight of thousands of street urchins, newsboys, and orphans. The public outcry helped charitable agencies build support for improving conditions for poor children. The Children's Aid Society organized the orphan trains, one of its most ambitious efforts. Between 1853 and 1929, over 120,000 orphaned or homeless New York City children were relocated to adoptive families in the Western United States.[3] And in 1886 a forerunner to today's multi-service shelter appeared when the country's first settlement house was founded on the city's Lower East Side, providing community and social services to impoverished families.[4]

At the time, the public placed the homeless into two categories: the "worthy poor," widows, children, and elderly who were offered relief at almshouses; and the "unworthy poor," wanderers and vagrants who were assigned to workhouses. Philanthropic organizations employed what they considered "scientific" methods to determine true need, and reformed a system they felt gave indiscriminate charity to "tramp menaces." For example, the city's wayfarer's lodges initiated a work requirement, where chopping a cord of wood (or for women shelter seekers, scrubbing floors) earned a night's lodging.[5]

The distinction between the "deserving" and the "undeserving" poor soon became meaningless with the massive economic downturn of the Great Depression. During the 1930s, thousands of New Yorkers lost their jobs and many became homeless, establishing shantytowns in city parks and vacant lots. No longer was it considered a moral failing to be found in a soup kitchen line. Even the language surrounding homelessness changed as the word "tramp" was replaced by the more neutral term "transient."[6]

Such widespread poverty prompted President Roosevelt to take action, and between 1933 and 1935 he unveiled the series of federal initiatives known as the New Deal. Among them were such make-work projects as the Civilian Conservation Corps (CCC), the Works Project Administration (WPA), and the Federal Transient Program (FTP). The latter served over thirteen-thousand people in New York City alone, providing treatment centers and work camps for homeless who wandered from place to place in search of employment. But one of the most significant New Deal achievements was the passage of the Social Security Act of 1936 and its Aid for Families with Dependent Children (AFDC) provision. AFDC gave states welfare grants earmarked for poor, single mothers and children, to be matched with state and local funds, enabling families to pay for their housing, food, and clothing. The country's first national welfare system was born.

A generation later, homelessness was more hidden, but still present in the city. In 1962, Michael Harrington's influential book, "The Other America: Poverty in the United States," helped to bring the enduring legacy of poverty back into public attention and heavily influenced President Lyndon Johnson's domestic policy agenda and his War on Poverty. His push to create or expand such programs as Medicaid, food stamps, Head Start, and AFDC contributed to a decline in the national poverty rate, from twenty-two percent (22%) in 1960 to approximately fourteen percent (14%) by 1969.[7] Ultimately, however, Johnson's vision for a "great society" was overshadowed and sidetracked as funding priorities shifted to the war in Vietnam.

The 1960s also witnessed a push for the de-institutionalization of psychiatric patients, eventually leading to the discharge of thousands of mentally ill people from public hospitals. Community-based housing and social services were an important part of their discharge plan, but they never came to be. While de-institutionalization appealed to liberals, who called for the individual freedom of patients, and conservatives, who sought to cut costs by shutting down hospitals, in New York, thousands of former patients ended up on city streets. Ironically, some of those former hospitals would eventually become homeless shelters, and the same clients who once had been patients receiving treatment there now lived in these facilities with few, if any, appropriate services.[8]

At the time, most of the homeless population was considered "chronically homeless" and "pathologically poor."[9] The typical homeless person in the city before 1980 was usually an unemployed single male adult, often with substance abuse and mental health problems. Temporarily displaced families with children

4

made up a far smaller group of the homeless population, but in recent years, their numbers have grown, so that the typical homeless person in New York City today is a young child.

A NEW POVERTY: THE NEW HOMELESS

But what happened in the 1980s? How did the shift from the "old homeless"—a mentally ill, substance abusing male—to the "new homeless"—young families and children—come about? How did emergency shelters fill beyond capacity and large old hotels become the much-criticized, crime-ridden "welfare hotels?" And why, after four mayors and numerous commissioners, could the city not get ahead of this crisis? Even after pouring billions of dollars into creating the most extensive shelter system in the country, it has been known for its inefficiency and inadequacy, even by those city officials who created it.

After twenty years, one has to wonder if a shelter has indeed become a home, and what lies ahead for homeless families today? Where do we go from here, and can things ever change? In the story that follows, we will explore these questions by examining the evolution of family homelessness in New York City and public policy responses through the 1980s, 1990s, and into the new millennium. Only by understanding the issue within this context can we begin a dialogue and offer a solution to begin to end family homelessness. In clear, down to earth language, this book presents a vision for real change.

NOTES

1. Coalition for the Homeless, "New York Kids Need Housing," 2003. Available at: <http://www.coalitionforthehomeless.org>.
2. Children's Aid Society, "History," Available at: <http://www.childrensaidsociety.org/about/history>.
3. Ibid.

4. United Neighborhood Houses, "Settlement House History," Available at: <http://www.unhny.org/about/settlement.cfm>.
5. Kenneth L Kusmer, *Down And Out and On the Road: The Homeless in American History* (New York: Oxford University Press, 2002) 74.
6. Ibid, 209.
7. U.S. Census Bureau, "Poverty," 2002. Available at: <http://www.census.gov/population/www/pop-profile/poverty.html>.
8. E. Fuller Torrey, "Stop the Madness," *Wall Street Journal* 18 July 1997.
9. Senator Daniel Patrick Moynihan's much-discussed report from 1965, *The Negro Family: The Case for National Action* helped popularize the notion of a "pathology" of poverty.

CHAPTER 1

THE EARLY 1980s
A First Response to a Growing Crisis

In many ways, the 1980s was a decade of contradictions. After years of blight and decay, New York City was finally beginning to flourish again. New immigrant groups and former suburbanites were establishing roots in the thriving urban metropolis, while world class businesses were staking their claim in the city's skyscrapers. Wall Street posted record gains, and the real estate market saw an unprecedented building boom. It was the era when New York moguls like Harry Helmsley and Donald Trump achieved fame, and the term "yuppie" (young urban professional) became a household word.

But this was also a decade in which the number of New Yorkers living in extreme poverty grew by alarming proportions. A crack epidemic ravaged the city's poorest neighborhoods, particularly Harlem, the South Bronx, Bushwick, and East New York. Crime was on the rise, as was the number of welfare recipients. By 1984, 927,000 people were receiving public assistance. And topping all of this, by 1989, the city faced a $1.8 billion budget deficit.[1]

The 1980s also marked the beginning of the modern homeless crisis, with the number of homeless parents and children seeking shelter growing by leaps and bounds. In 1982, 950 families were in the city's emergency shelter system; by 1988, that figure had climbed to over five-thousand, an increase of five hundred percent (500%) (see Figure 1.1).[2] A small portion of the city's homeless had always consisted of families, who had usually been

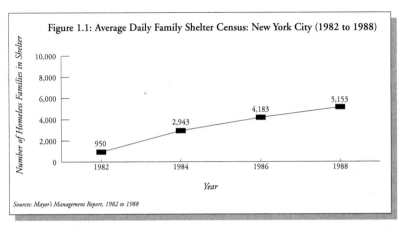

Figure 1.1: Average Daily Family Shelter Census: New York City (1982 to 1988)

Number of Homeless Families in Shelter

Year

Sources: Mayor's Management Report, 1982 to 1988

displaced as a result of some unforeseen event, such as a fire or illness; they were simply temporarily down on their luck. But in the 1980s, the situation changed as living in a shelter took on negative connotations, becoming synonymous with dependence and evoking the myth of the welfare queen.

Moreover, New York City was completely unprepared for the steady stream of homeless families. They presented an entirely new challenge to the city's conscience, budget, and capacity to serve its citizens. By the end of the 1980s, with thousands of families relying on shelters, the city scrambled for a solution. At the same time, a debate arose over the possible causes for such an exponential increase: was it a lagging economy, cuts in social services, or a lack of affordable housing?

THE ECONOMY

The national economic recession in the early eighties left its mark on New York City and increased the number of families living in poverty. As the national unemployment rate reached eight percent (8%), the city's climbed to over ten percent (10.5%), a ten-year high.[3] Especially hard hit was the manufacturing sector, an industry that had traditionally provided a viable employment avenue for New Yorkers with little or no schooling. Meanwhile, the minimum wage remained constant at $3.35 between 1981 and 1990, despite a forty-eight percent (48%) rise in the cost of living.[4]

As real incomes fell, the number of families living in poverty rose so that by 1983, twenty-seven percent (27%) of New York City renters lived below the poverty line, up from just over twenty-two percent (22.5%) in 1977, with the Bronx having the highest number, thirty-six percent (36.3%) (see Figure 1.2).[5] Over the same period, the poverty rate for the city's children jumped from twenty-one (21%) to thirty percent (30%).[6] By the mid 1980s, when the economy finally began to recover and flourish, it was the middle and upper classes, rather than low-income families, that reaped the gains of the so-called Reagan economy.

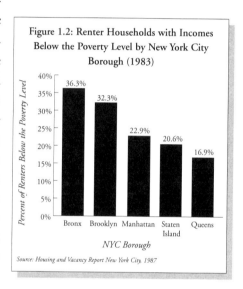

Figure 1.2: Renter Households with Incomes Below the Poverty Level by New York City Borough (1983)

Source: *Housing and Vacancy Report New York City, 1987*

SOCIAL SERVICE CUTS

Just as many New Yorkers were facing unemployment and poverty, a series of public policy shifts were underway that would affect the level of available social service benefits. During the economic recession of the early eighties, the Reagan administration began to restructure the scope and delivery of social services and cut back the role of the federal government. In fact, between 1980 and 1990, the federal government significantly increased spending on the military while dramatically reducing funding for social pro-

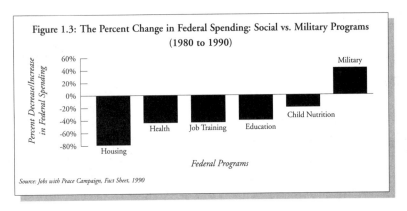

Figure 1.3: The Percent Change in Federal Spending: Social vs. Military Programs (1980 to 1990)

Federal Programs

Source: *Jobs with Peace Campaign, Fact Sheet, 1990*

grams (see Figure 1.3).

Beginning with the Omnibus Budget Reconciliation Act of 1981, the administration drastically cut the budget for many traditional entitlement programs and delegated much of its social welfare responsibilities to the states. As a result, benefits for poor families, such as Aid to Families with Dependent Children (AFDC), food stamps, and housing assistance, were sharply reduced. Between 1970 and 1981, an average of seventy-two percent (72%) of all poor American children received AFDC; by the end of 1987, only fifty-four percent (54%) were receiving such assistance.[7]

Other critical services also evaporated as programs addressing drug abuse, teen pregnancy, and domestic violence were eliminated. Without federal support, low-income individuals slipped further into poverty and their drug-ravaged neighborhoods continued to deteriorate. Although the city and state did what they could to make up the difference, they had their own budget deficits to grapple with.

LACK OF AFFORDABLE HOUSING

At the same time the federal government was scaling back entitlement programs and benefits, it was also withdrawing from its low-income housing efforts. The Reagan Administration's

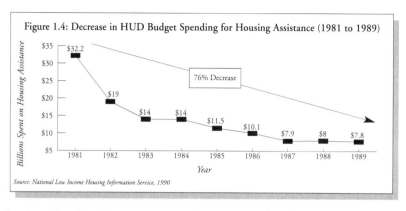

Figure 1.4: Decrease in HUD Budget Spending for Housing Assistance (1981 to 1989)

Source: National Low Income Housing Information Service, 1990

budget for the Department of Housing and Urban Development (HUD) fell from over $30 billion in 1981 to under $8 billion in 1989 (see Figure 1.4).[8] In New York City, those numbers translated into a $1.5 billion drop in aid.[9]

Moreover, the extremely competitive rental market in New York further exacerbated the decline in low-income housing resources. On block after city block, tenements and dilapidated buildings were being demolished to make way for more upscale units. Between 1984 and 1987, there was a fifty-five percent (55%) drop in the number of units available for less than $300 per month, while at the same time there was a one hundred and ninety one percent (191%) increase in units renting for $1,000 or more (see Table 1.1).[10] Many of the buildings slated for either demolition or renovation were single room occupancy units, or SROs. For very poor individuals, these humble one-room lodgings with communal bathrooms were the traditional last stopgap before homelessness.

Even for middle class New Yorkers, affordable housing was difficult to find. The standard measure of an affordable rent, as defined by the U.S. Department of Housing and Urban Development, is no more than thirty percent (30%) of a person's monthly income. When looking for an apartment, many New Yorkers found that not going above this so-called reasonable threshold was difficult, if not impossible. The issue was even more problematic for low-income families, for whom using the major-ity of their income for rent was a fact of life. Nationwide in 1985, more than seventy-nine percent (79%) of low income renters paid thirty-five percent (35%) or more of their monthly income towards housing, and

Table 1.1: Available Vacant Units by Monthly Contract Rent: New York City (1984 and 1987)			
Contract Rent	Available Units		Percent Change
	1984	1987	
Low Income Units			
< $300	12,856	5,836	-55%
$300 to $399	6,535	10,115	+55%
Total	**19,400**	**15,951**	**-18%**
Moderate Income Units			
$400 to $499	3,576	7,843	+119%
$500 to $599	1,833	5,556	+203%
Total	**5,409**	**13,399**	**+148%**
Upper Middle Income & **Luxury Units**			
$600 to $749	1,450	5,176	+257%
$750 to $999	2,261	4,642	+105%
$1,000 >	1,318	3,831	+191%
Total	**5,029**	**13,640**	**+171%**

Source: Housing and Vacancy Report New York City, 1987

fifty-five percent (55%) paid more than sixty percent (60%), often placing renters on the brink of homelessness.[11]

CONTRIBUTING FACTORS

Beyond these structural causes, there were other factors that fueled the dramatic growth of the shelter population. In the 1980s, crack cocaine emerged as the drug of choice in New York's low-income neighborhoods, and Acquired Immune Deficiency Syndrome (AIDS) became a rampant threat for intravenous drug users.

It is difficult to identify a single tangible reason why families became homeless; often it was due to a combination of factors. In many cases, drug addiction, domestic violence, and medical prob-lems had a simultaneous impact on families. In the downward spi-ral of poverty, cuts in social services, a lack of affordable housing and economic trends only exacerbated pre-existing conditions. Without housing and employment options, families became the new clients of an over-stretched New York City shelter system.

THE EMERGENCY SHELTER BUILD-UP

In the city's scramble to provide shelter services, early efforts focused on the short-term emergency component rather than the need for more affordable housing, social services, or preventive strategies. The situation grew so frantic that some shelter officials referred to long-range planning as "what will we do with these homeless families tomorrow night."[12] In what could be seen as a case study in poor planning, the city's major initiative was simply to provide shelter clients with a bed and a meal. While this may have been a reasonable response given the political and economic realities of the time, it did little to address the root causes of the problem.

The city's first line of defense was to continue a policy begun in the 1970s of placing homeless families in vacant hotel rooms when shelter space was exhausted.[13] In 1983, the city even began placements in hotels outside of New York City, including Westchester County, Long Island, and New Jersey, where over three hundred families were placed in hotels in Secaucus, Union City, and Newark alone, creating an uproar in inter-state relations, with New Jersey Governor Kean decrying the policy as "the height of irresponsibility."[14]

In response, the city turned to using readily available local facilities, such as gymnasiums and auditoriums within the city, to create large congregate family shelters. Rows of metal sleeping cots were assembled in these barracks-style locations with the assumption that each family might only stay for two or three days. Yet not only did they stay much longer, these congregate shelters eventually became much more chaotic and unsafe than anyone had imagined.[15]

The most infamous example was the two hundred and ten bed

Roberto Clemente facility, opened in 1983 and located in a gymnasium on the grounds of the Roberto Clemente State Park in the Bronx. Privacy was non-existent: families had no secure place to leave belongings, bathrooms were communal, and the lights were kept on all night. Criticism of this shelter came from all sides: community members and state officials who could no longer utilize a part of this state park, homeless advocates who objected to the shelter's overcrowded conditions, and city officials who found the $70,000 per family annual cost outrageous.[16]

RESPONSES FROM THE PUBLIC AND THE COURTS

At the same time that New Yorkers were becoming aware of the conditions at congregate shelters like Roberto Clemente, the rest of America was learning about the city's homeless epidemic. Numerous articles and media reports chronicled the plight of people living on steam grates and park benches, and the word "homeless" was coined to describe this new population—a more sensitive term than the earlier monikers of "tramp," "bum," and "hobo."[17] And New York's growing shelter infrastructure even inspired the false belief that homeless individuals from outside the region were coming to the city just to take advantage of its emergency shelter services.

There was also confusion concerning the more hidden problem of homeless families. Since parents and children tended to go to city shelters rather than sleep on park benches or the streets, their situation was less visible, and most people did not know that a homeless person could also be a child. In contrast, the public seemed well aware and highly critical of the large numbers of single mothers receiving welfare benefits, with over 740,000 women on AFDC in New York City in 1984. They were portrayed in the popular press as "welfare queens," lazy women breeding babies in pursuit of the next welfare check.[18] The reality, of course, was quite different; these were young women with young children, caught in the vicious cycle of poverty; and having more children was often an unplanned by-product of their environment. Nonetheless, young, poor, single mothers received more condemnation than compassion in the press.

However, the case of homeless families was recognized by a small group of advocates who fought for better shelter conditions by suing the city for guaranteed shelter for the homeless. Throughout the 1980s, the pro-bono lawyers of the Legal Aid Society sparred with city officials in a series of court battles. Claiming conditions at the intake centers and the shelters were inhumane, they monitored the treatment of individual homeless families, and filed legal petitions on their behalf. On the opposite side, city officials grumbled that the constant battles with Legal Aid were creating bureaucratic red tape and preventing them from implementing real reforms.

Ultimately, the Legal Aid Society won a series of court victories that made significant changes in city shelter rules and established New York's right to shelter laws. In 1981, Callahan v. Carey affirmed the city's obligation to shelter single men and established minimum health and safety standards for shelters. The same right was extended to homeless women a year later with Eldredge v. Koch. And in 1986, the McCain v. Koch decision gave the right to shelter to homeless families with children and prohibited the city from consigning families to remain overnight in welfare offices.[19] Together, these rulings made great strides in improving conditions for homeless New Yorkers and guaranteed them the right to shelter, a mandate unique among urban areas. The order of the court decisions also demonstrated the widespread public perception of homelessness; men, the most visible segment of the population, were granted the right to shelter first; followed by women; and finally families, who were hidden away from public view and consequently not given much consideration.

The continuing growth of homelessness, the ensuing emergency responses, and the legal fights of the 1980s together laid the groundwork for today's shelter infrastructure. Through legal and political efforts, New York City shelters would evolve into a system unmatched by any other American city, most of which rely on private charities to provide shelter. Today, New York allocates over $636 million to homeless services annually, with $356 million earmarked for families alone.[20] Nonetheless, we will see that the city's emergency efforts, band-aid solutions, and knee-jerk legal positions only exacerbated a growing problem.

NOTES

1. New York City Human Resources Administration, *Mayor's Management Report* (New York: New York City Human Resources Administration, 1985) 505.
2. *Mayor's Management Report, 1988*, 535.
3. L. Mishel, J. Bernstein, and J. Schmitt, *The State of Working America: 1998-1999* (Washington, DC: Economic Policy Institute, 1999) 208. New York State Department of Labor, Available at: <http://www.labor.state.ny.us>.
4. Mishel, Bernstein, and Schmitt, 208.
5. Michael Stegman, *Housing and Vacancy Report: New York City* (New York: Department of Housing, Preservation, and Development, 1987).
6. Annie E. Casey Foundation, "Kids Count," Available at: <http://www.aecf.org>
7. Martha Burt, *Over the Edge: The Growth of Homelessness in the 1980s* (New York: Russell Sage Foundation, 1992) 83-87.
   R.B. Reich, "As the World Turns," *New Republic* (issue 3876) (1989) 28.
   L.K. Mihaly, *Homeless Families: Failed Policies and Young Victims* (Washington, DC: Children's Defense Fund, Jan. 1991) 14.
   S.A. Hewlett, *When the Bough Breaks: The Cost of Neglecting*

Our Children (New York: Basic Books, 1991) 45, 148.

8. National Jobs With Peace Campaign, *Fact Sheet* (Boston: National Jobs With Peace Campaign, 1990).

9. National Low Income Housing Coalition, *Changing Priorities: The Federal Budget and Housing Assistance 1976-2007* (Washington, DC: National Low Income Housing Coalition, 1990) 10.

10. Stegman, *Housing and Vacancy Report: New York City.*

11. Paul H. Leonard, Cushing N. Dolbeare, Edward B. Lazare, *A Place to Call Home: The Crisis in Housing for the Poor* (Washington, DC: Center for Budget and Policy Priorities, 1989) Table 1.

12. Larry Schatt, former Assistant Commissioner of Homeless Services, personal interview, 8 Feb. 2002.

13. Ken Murphy, former Commissioner of Homeless Services, personal interview, 26 Feb. 2002.

14. *Mayor's Management Report, 1983*, 440; "Cuomo Makes Visit to Homeless," *New York Times* 19 Dec. 1985.

15. Ken Murphy, personal interview.

16. Cynthia Nix, "Housing Family in a Shelter Costs the City $70,000 Per Year, " *New York Times* 7 Mar. 1986.

17. See Kenneth L. Kusmer, *Down and Out, On The Road: The Homeless In American History* (New York: Oxford University Press, 2002) for a further exploration of the various monikers for homeless individuals.

18. David Zucchino, *The Myth of the Welfare Queen,* (New York: Touchstone, Simon and Shulster, 1997) 65. According to David Zucchino, Ronald Reagan helped bring the term into popular consciousness during his 1976 presidential campaign. Reagan mentioned in a speech that a Chicago welfare mother had allegedly cheated the system, which gave her a "tax-free income" of "over $150,000." It was the newspapers reporting the story that dubbed her "the welfare queen."

19. Coalition for the Homeless, *The Right to Shelter for Homeless New Yorkers: Twenty Years and Counting,* (New York: Coalition for the Homeless, Jun. 2002). *Callahan v. Carey* was filed as a class action lawsuit in 1979. In 1981, it was settled as a court consent decree guaranteeing a right to shelter for homeless men in New York City, and establishing minimum health and safety standards for shelters. *Eldredge v. Koch* was filed in 1982; it argued for equal rights and standards for homeless women. The case was eventually included in the *Callahan* decree and extended the right to shelter to women. *McCain v. Koch* was filed in 1986 on behalf of homeless families with children. The city was ordered to provide emergency housing to homeless families with children, and prohibited from leaving families to remain overnight in welfare offices by the Appellate Division of the State Supreme Court. *McCain* extended the right to shelter to homeless families with children. In 1990, *McCain* was amended, and now stipulated that the city must phase out the use of noncompliant welfare hotels and overnight shelter beds, the city must provide permanent housing units for homeless families with children, and the city must operate a 24-hour emergency intake center for homeless families. For more information, see <http://www.coalitionforthehomeless.org>.

20. New York City Human Resources Administration, *Mayor's Management Report Preliminary Fiscal* (New York: New York City Human Resources Administration 2003). Historically, the federal government has provided fifty percent (50%) of homeless funding, with the state and city governments each contributing twenty-five percent (25%). Michael Goodwin, "State is Penalizing City Over Shelter Conditions," *New York Times* 21 Dec. 1983.

CHAPTER 2

THE MID 1980S
Emergency Efforts: The EAU and Welfare Hotels

The series of court decrees in the early eighties, guaranteeing the right to shelter for every man, woman, and child in New York City, put enormous pressure on city officials to deal with the growing homeless crisis, and fostered the hasty implementation of quick-fix solutions. Their entire focus was devoted to finding short-term policies.

At the same time, in order to deter other poorly housed families from entering the shelter system, officials sought to keep temporary shelter arrangements from becoming too comfortable, resulting in a costly shelter infrastructure with deteriorating facilities ill-equipped for the needs of thousands of infants and young children.

EMERGENCY ASSISTANCE UNITS

A family's journey through the shelter system began with intake, either at the local welfare office, known as Income Maintenance Centers (IMs) or, in the evening, at Emergency Assistance Units (EAUs). The EAUs were a unique concept at the time: four intake offices where families could register and then be referred for short-term shelter.[1] The idea was to first assess a family's needs, and then to place them in an appropriate emergency housing setting.

In reality, the EAUs came to function as overcrowded, chaotic holding pens, where families would wait for an initial conditional shelter placement for anywhere from four to twenty hours.

Even after that assignment, many families endured multiple back-and-forth trips between a few hours sleep in a temporary shelter and whole days spent at an EAU awaiting placement. Before McCain v. Koch prohibited the practice, families unable to secure a placement before nightfall often spent the night sleeping on chairs or the floor at one of these centers.[2]

The EAUs were part of a system plagued by troubles from the very start. In the early years of operation, there was no comprehensive database to track placements, or even to determine eligibility. Anyone claiming to be homeless was entitled to shelter, regardless of income level or housing need. As a result, the EAUs were almost always backlogged, and many times even open to fraud. Some families who had alternate living arrangements simply wanted a private hotel room for the weekend. Others intentionally entered the system just to get their names on the public housing waiting list, since homeless families received priority placements there.[3] All in all the EAUs did not work very well.

TIER I FACILITIES

In 1986, just as EAU operations were being reorganized, New York State formalized a set of shelter regulations to ensure uniform safety standards and services. As a result, shelters began to be categorized, with large congregate sites like Roberto Clemente classified as Tier I facilities. These congregate, Tier I sites represented the least desirable housing option for homeless families, and it was common for parents to refuse placement there.

Since congregate facilities were so unappealing, city leaders actually hoped their conditions might deter families from entering the system to begin with.[4] A New York City Council report in 1986 challenged such deterrence theories, concluding that the worst facilities had the longest length of stay, while those with better conditions and enhanced social services had better success in moving families to long-term affordable housing; the practice continued nonetheless.[5]

Some city officials shared homeless families' dislike of these facilities; in one mayoral report, they were derided as "wasteful, ineffective, and inefficient."[6] Considering the cost of food, maintenance, and security, housing just one family in a Tier I facility could cost as much as $145 per night.[7] Moreover, life in these large shelters did not include practical housing search assistance or comprehensive social services. As a result, the city eventually began to scale back congregate placements, so that by the end of 1986, just eight percent (8%) of the homeless family population, roughly 330 families, were residing in Tier I sites (see Figure 2.1).[8]

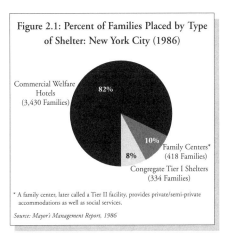

Figure 2.1: Percent of Families Placed by Type of Shelter: New York City (1986)

Commercial Welfare Hotels (3,430 Families) 82%

10% Family Centers* (418 Families)

8% Congregate Tier I Shelters (334 Families)

* A family center, later called a Tier II facility, provides private/semi-private accommodations as well as social services.

Source: *Mayor's Management Report, 1986*

WELFARE HOTELS

At the same time, 3,400 families, or eighty-two percent (82%) of the homeless family population, were living in so-called commercial welfare hotels.[9] These hotels were a slight step up from congregate shelters, but still substandard. They began to represent all the failings of the city's shelter policy and ultimately inspired a surge of public controversy.[10]

With little fanfare, the city had begun working on an ad-hoc basis with willing hotel owners who could simply rent them a couple of rooms, floors, or even the entire site to house homeless families. The venture was completely private, and managed by the hotel at a cost of up to $99 per room per night. Rates were determined individually with each site, averaging $53 per room or $17 for the head of household and $12 for each additional family member.[11] One month's rent was defined as 28 days in order to avoid a legal technicality (Local Law 4) that would give residents who stayed for more than 30 days the same anti-eviction rights as apartment tenants.[12] By 1986, the cost to house a family of four at a hotel for one year was estimated at nearly $20,000, not including food and services, and the city's total bill for such placements had climbed to $72 million annually.[13]

When families arrived at these hotels they found cramped, vermin-infested rooms, where narrow hallways and stairs were the only play areas available for their children. And despite their high price tag, these facilities offered neither the typical amenities of a hotel nor any supportive or educational services, with only one visiting social worker assigned to dozens of families.[14] The larger hotels, including the infamous Martinique and Holland, quickly became hotbeds of criminal activity, with various "friends" and unwelcome "guests" using them as the base for thriving drug and prostitution rings. In this atmosphere, where anarchy reigned and security was minimal, safety became a constant concern for families with young children.

HOTEL SCRUTINY: THE MEDIA'S ROLE

With controversy over hotels growing, newspapers began to expose some of the suspect practices of a chaotic and mismanaged system. At the time, the *New York Times* offices were across the street from the Hotel Carter in midtown Manhattan, a hotel that was openly criticized by the city itself for its "consistently low rate of compliance in correcting health and safety violations."[15] The Holland Hotel, on West 42nd street, was in turn cited for over a thousand health and building violations, including no hot water. They were fined $40,000 by the Environmental Control Board and were later found to have unpaid water and sewer bills totaling

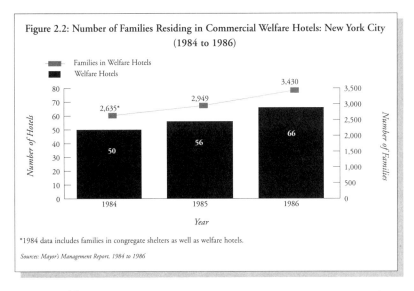

Figure 2.2: Number of Families Residing in Commercial Welfare Hotels: New York City (1984 to 1986)

*1984 data includes families in congregate shelters as well as welfare hotels.

Sources: Mayor's Management Report, 1984 to 1986

$56,805.[16] Nonetheless, the city continued to use these hotels to house homeless families (see Figure 2.2).

Equally disturbing was the fact that the hotel owners were reaping tremendous profits from the city. For example, the owner of the Holland Hotel was earning $6 million a year, with a $4 million profit at the public's expense. In fact, welfare hotels were becoming so lucrative that many of the city's single room occupancy (SRO) buildings, which traditionally offered low rent lodging for the poor, converted to hotels to reap greater profits. [17]

Ongoing publicity eventually revealed the tremendous hold that hotel proprietors had over city officials, who were under intense pressure to abide by right to shelter regulations and house homeless families. The city had little control or negotiating power over the hotels, and the most basic of reforms were met with resistance. For example, in 1985 the city attempted to give hotel families their own small refrigerators for nutritional and sanitary reasons. Since rooms did not come equipped with kitchen facilities, the city provided each family with a restaurant allowance. But having a cold place to keep food, baby formula, and medicine was a necessity for mothers with young children, some of whom, out of desperation, stored baby bottles on windowsills.

In response, the city's Human Resources Administration purchased several hundred small refrigerators for mothers with newborns or late in pregnancy, but the hotel managers refused to allow them to be installed unless the city relaxed its health inspections, thus reducing violations. A compromise was reached and the city agreed to pay an extra fee per room per week to cover expenses from maintenance and replacements. In the end, the city was being nickeled and dimed by these operators at every turn, and families with children became the pawns in what were essentially financial shakedowns. Such sagas generated both sympathy for the mothers and disgust towards the hotel owners, who leveraged the issue to earn more money at the public's expense.

Eventually, media coverage led to the widespread realization that the fifty-five welfare hotels were the city's main homeless policy strategy. People were outraged that the program wasted so much taxpayer money and that the system could "dump" so many poor families on certain neighborhoods. For middle and upper class Manhattanites, this was a particular threat. Twenty-six percent (26%) of homeless families were concentrated in eight welfare hotels from Broadway to 3rd Avenue between 21st and 35th Streets, traditionally one of Manhattan's more upscale neighborhoods.[18] Ultimately, it was this initial outcry that brought the first real reforms, as the city was forced to examine new policy avenues. Unfortunately, as we will see in later chapters, these reforms were ineffective in stopping for-profit housing for the homeless. In fact, the system may have come full circle, with history now on the verge of repeating itself.

FROM EMERGENCY RESPONSES TO LONG-TERM SOLUTIONS

The cost of sheltering homeless families was growing exponentially; between 1978 and 1985, the city's budget allocation of aggregate state, local, and federal funds rose from $8 million to over $100 million.[19] The primary focus remained on "emergency" efforts since the administration believed that permanent housing efforts would create incentives for families to enter the shelter system. But with the tremendous controversies generated by emergency approaches like congregate shelters and welfare hotels, the Koch administration had no choice but to push for new residential options for homeless families.

Although the city did not have much land on which to build, it could boast ownership of thousands of empty buildings. By 1986, the city was the landlord for 53,000 occupied units and 49,000 vacant ones obtained *in rem*, foreclosed upon as the result of non-payment of taxes.[20] In 1983, the Department of Housing Preservation and Development (HPD) had initiated a large-scale program to convert 4,474 *in rem* apartments into low-income housing for the homeless. Although this had helped expand the supply of available units, it was criticized for only renovating individual apartments, often leaving the building's shell, hallways, and stairways in serious disrepair.

As a result, the Koch administration took a second look at the city's supply of *in rem* buildings and settled on a ten-year, $5.1 billion effort to build up New York City's reserve of permanent low-income housing for homeless families, a plan known as Housing New York.[21] Part of this effort was Koch's Special Initiatives Program (SIP): a four-year plan to completely rehabilitate 5,600 units of *in rem* housing into low-income apartments. The first wave of SIP was a plan to move 750 families from the ten largest hotels into affordable housing, but city officials soon discovered that the implementation of such a plan would take some time. Although things were changing, it would not be until the next mayoral administration that SIP housing would become available, while the number of families entering the shelter system was increasing daily.[22]

THE MOVE TOWARDS TRANSITIONAL HOUSING

With the demand for apartments far exceeding the supply, homeless families were languishing in "short term" shelters and hotels for an average of fourteen months.[23] Clearly, a better residential model was needed, one that would bridge the gap between homelessness and independent living. City officials and advocates alike contemplated a number of alternate approaches, including paying homeless families to "double up" with relatives, sending New York City's homeless families to live in vacant apartments throughout New York State, and even establishing mobile home campgrounds throughout the five boroughs.[24]

But the approach that officials considered the most cost-effective was to create "family centers," also known as Tier II transitional facilities, operated by non-profit organizations. In the years to come, the city would vigorously pursue the development of these centers, which would offer smaller, more home-like supportive living settings to help families move towards independence. Their operational success has made them the dominant form of family shelter in the city today.

NOTES

1. The EAU in Queens closed in 1993 and the Brooklyn location closed in 1994.
2. Larry Schatt, personal interview, 8 Feb. 2002.
3. Ibid.
4. Barbara Basler, "Koch Limits Using Welfare Hotels," *New York Times* 17 Dec. 1985.
5. Jonathan Kozol, *Rachel and Her Children* (New York: Crown, 1988) endnotes.
6. New York City Commission on the Homeless, *The Way Home: A New Direction in Social Policy* (New York: New York City Commission on the Homeless, 1992) 13.
7. New York City Commission on the Homeless, *The Way*

Home, 110. The $145 per family per night is an estimate put forth by the New York City Commission on the Homeless and is significantly less than the $70,000 per family per year mentioned earlier. The larger figure is specific to the Roberto Clemente shelter; the other refers to Tier Is in general.

8. New York City Human Resources Administration, *Mayor's Management Report* (New York: New York City Human Resources Administration, 1986).

9. Ibid.

10. The notion of using hotels to handle the occasional nightly overflow of homeless families was not a new one for city officials. In 1971 the administration of then Mayor John Lindsay placed a homeless family in the exclusive Waldorf-Astoria hotel for $77 per night, an experiment promptly abandoned following a media outcry over such an outrageous expense. Clara Hemphill, "The High Price of Sheltering City's Homeless," *Newsday* 2 Dec. 1988.

11. Manhattan Borough President's Task Force on Housing and Homeless Families, *A Shelter Is Not A Home* (New York: Manhattan Borough President's Task Force on Housing for Homeless Families, Mar. 1987) 26.

12. According to Local Law #4.

13. Manhattan Borough President's Task Force on Housing and Homeless Families, *A Shelter Is Not A Home,* 26. Not including food and services, the direct shelter cost in 1986 was $19,716 annually at the Martinique Hotel and $21,900 at the Allerton Hotel.

14. Manhattan Borough President's Task Force on Housing and Homeless Families, *A Shelter Is Not A Home,* 115. According to this report, there was one caseworker for every sixty families at some welfare hotels.

15. Michael Goodwin, "State is Penalizing City Over Shelter Conditions," *New York Times* 21 Dec. 1983.

16. Barbara Basler, "Welfare Hotels Sued Over Taxes," *New York Times* 27 Dec. 1985.

17. Crystal Nix, "Profits of Welfare Hotels Placed at $3M," *New York Times* 23 Nov. 1985.

18. "New York Barred from Placing Needy Families in Midtown Hotels," *Associated Press* 21 Dec. 1986.

19. Ralph da Costa Nunez, *The New Poverty; Homeless Families in America* (New York: Insight Books, 1996) 34.

20. *In rem* is a legal term referring to an action or judgment against a property. In 1976, the city began foreclosing properties that were one year in tax arrears, in contrast to an earlier policy that allowed for a three-year grace period. The result was a sharp increase in the number of foreclosed and abandoned properties in the late 1970s. Housing First! "The Housing New York Ten Year Plan," Available at: <http://www.housingfirst.net/policypaper_app_b.html>

21. Laura Castro, "Bankers Trust Funds Housing for Homeless," *Newsday* 19 Aug. 1990.

22. Thomas Lueck, "Breaking Ground in Housing Policy," *New York Times* 30 Apr. 1989.

23. Manhattan Borough President's Task Force on Housing for Homeless Families, *A Shelter Is Not A Home,* 2.

24. Michael Goodwin, "Carol Bellamy Fights Sharing of Apartments of Homeless Families," *New York Times* 28 Jun. 1984.

CHAPTER 3

THE LATE 1980s AND EARLY 1990s
Old Problems, New Strategies

The late eighties and early nineties was a time of great transition for homeless policy in New York City. Leadership changed from three-term Mayor Ed Koch to Mayor David Dinkins in 1990. At the same time, homeless service delivery was also evolving, particularly with the creation of a new city agency, the Department of Homeless Services (DHS).

By 1987, the number of homeless families in the shelter system had grown to roughly 5,000, and increased to almost 5,700 by 1993 (see Figure 3.1).[1] Each year, the emergency assistance units (EAUs) grew more crowded, with families waiting all day and through the night for placement (see Figure 3.2). Every evening, officials performed frantic searches to find available hotel

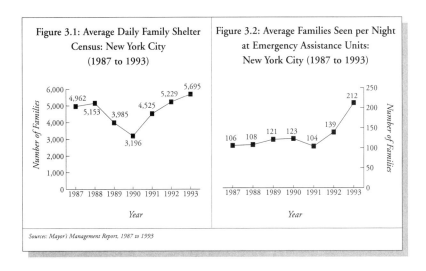

Figure 3.1: Average Daily Family Shelter Census: New York City (1987 to 1993)

Figure 3.2: Average Families Seen per Night at Emergency Assistance Units: New York City (1987 to 1993)

Sources: Mayor's Management Report, 1987 to 1993

rooms, apartments, or shelter slots, often of questionable quality.[2]

When it came to addressing this crisis, Mayors Koch and Dinkins shared a commitment to helping homeless families. When Koch was in office, the crisis was so nascent that the focus was on providing emergency beds. But by the Dinkins era, the focus had moved away from congregate shelters and welfare hotels towards transitional Tier II facilities and ultimately to permanent, low-income housing.

For Mayor Dinkins, this strategy was pursued in part to fulfill his campaign promise to put welfare hotels out of business. In 1989, 1,500 families were living in these hotels; by 1990, the number was down to 150.[3] The goal of arriving at "zero day," when no more homeless families would reside in hotels, seemed well within reach (see Figure 3.3).[4] But even this success was blunted by a continuing tide of incoming families, and by 1992, over a thousand were again living in hotels.[5]

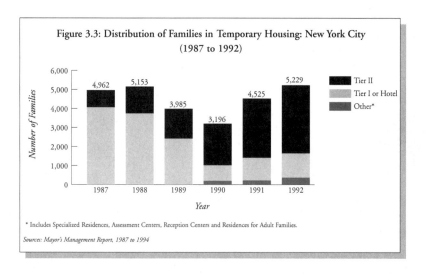

Figure 3.3: Distribution of Families in Temporary Housing: New York City (1987 to 1992)

* Includes Specialized Residences, Assessment Centers, Reception Centers and Residences for Adult Families.

Sources: *Mayor's Management Report, 1987 to 1994*

A New Agency

In his efforts to confront the crisis in a meaningful way, Mayor Dinkins created a Blue Ribbon Commission on Homelessness in 1992 to evaluate the city's existing shelter system and to come up with new ways to improve homeless policy. A collaboration of city officials, public policy experts, homeless advocates, and non-profit administrators met for six months and issued a series of recommendations in their report "The Way Home: A New Direction in Social Policy."[6] The Commission argued that the existing shelter system was only exacerbating the problems of the persistently poor and dependent. It recommended that the city provide both housing and services to homeless people, concluding that both are equally necessary.[7] It also called for contracting transitional housing to non-profit service providers and developing more small service-rich transitional facilities.

Finally, Dinkins' Commission proposed the creation of an entirely new agency, responsible for the implementation of their recommendations and the operation and oversight of all homeless services.[8] What evolved was the Department of Homeless Services (DHS), absorbing the Agency for Adult and Family Services and the Mayor's Office of Homeless Services (established by Koch in 1986). In 1993, DHS began to assume responsibility for the city's homeless from the Human Resources Administration (HRA), taking over shelter provision and services for homeless families and individuals, as well as the development of citywide homeless policy.[9]

Transitioning to Tier II

The recommendations from the Dinkins report confirmed what many advocates and city officials had long understood—the shelter system desperately needed reform. Emergency shelter measures and welfare hotels were costly, dangerous, and doing little to help families escape poverty. Even after families finally left the shelter system for a housing placement, their reprieve from homelessness was often short-lived. A 1992 study by the Department of Housing Preservation and Development found a high recidivism rate within the homeless population, with fifty percent (50%) of the families reapplying for housing after having received a placement on a prior occasion.[10] Any new shelter initiative would have to target the challenges homeless families faced in living stable, independent lives.

As often was the case with homeless policy during this era, the courts set the ball rolling. A 1990 consent order decree in the McCain v. Koch decision outlawed the use of welfare hotels and congregate Tier I shelters for families, leading the City Council to mandate the closing of all Tier I sites by 1991.[11] In response, the city began the frantic process of converting hospitals, schools, and other facilities into Tier II shelters, as well as designing and building new ones. Nonetheless, with the ongoing surge of new homeless families, the goal of closing all Tier I shelters was not achieved until 1993.[12]

Tier Is were no longer the first stop on the road to shelter, but city officials could not ensure that every family would receive a Tier II placement, a problem that remains until this day. Still, by 1994, seventy percent (70%) of the city's homeless families had moved into Tier II units, at a cost of roughly $33 per person per day, compared to $145 per family per day in a Tier I site.[13]

As city officials began focusing more on policy and regulations than shelter operations, they called upon the non-profit sector to design and operate the Tier II system. At the time, non-profit shelter operators were permitted to selectively admit clients into their facilities. Consequently, some city administrators objected to awarding them contracts, charging that they achieved favorable outcomes by selecting the most promising families from the pool of homeless applicants, a process known as creaming. The Human

Resources Administration in particular argued that non-profit transitional housing operators creamed the smallest, least troubled families, leaving the city to deal with the "problem" ones.[14]

But despite these charges, experience showed that these organizations could provide technical expertise and efficient services without a complicated bureaucracy or a high price tag. As a result, the city began to withdraw from a direct role in servicing the homeless, and by the late 1980s, private non-profit groups became the primary service providers. These organizations would be the ones to further develop the Tier II model in response to families' needs, ultimately influencing the evolution of homeless policy in New York.

With different providers managing different types of facilities, the first transitional shelters had varied features, including communal kitchens, bathrooms, or living areas. By the late 1980s, the definition of a transitional city facility became more uniform, with the advent of the state's Part 900 regulations governing what a "Tier II" shelter would look like. According to those regulations, Tier II family shelters were defined as facilities providing shelter and services to ten or more homeless families. They were required to offer, at a minimum, private rooms, three meals a day, child care, health services, assessment and referral to services, as well as guidance in the permanent housing placement process. The regulations also set the average length of stay at six months, in reality families would stay significantly longer.[15]

Local Resistance: Not In My Back Yard

In the move towards transitional housing, the city administration and the non-profit providers encountered strong resistance from neighborhood groups. Where Tier I shelters were operated in empty armories, old schools, and welfare hotels located wherever they could be found, Tier II housing was meant to be spread across existing neighborhoods in all five boroughs. It required

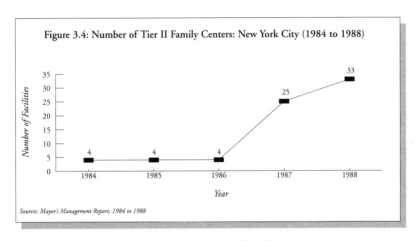

Figure 3.4: Number of Tier II Family Centers: New York City (1984 to 1988)

Sources: Mayor's Management Report, 1984 to 1988

both new construction and a new reality for local residents, who might come to know the homeless as the people next door. Not surprisingly, the not-in-my-backyard (NIMBY) attitude emerged, as community boards and neighborhood associations waged opposition against proposed facilities, arguing that Tier II shelters would lower property values. Lawsuits backed by local politicians, coupled with intense media coverage, became stumbling blocks in the campaign to build or rehabilitate new transitional housing.

Nonetheless, by 1988, there were a total of thirty-three Tier II family centers, up from only four in 1986 (see Figure 3.4).[16] These facilities proved to be successful models of transitional, non-profit operated housing. More homelike than congregate shelters, but with more supervision and services than private apartments and housing projects, Tier IIs helped families build a foundation to move towards independent living. They mirrored models used successfully in supervised housing for youth, the mentally ill, and the elderly.

STEPS FORWARD, STEPS BACK

Tier II shelters were designed with the concept that they could be converted into permanent housing once the homeless crisis was over. But by the early 1990s, the situation was nowhere near ending, and despite efforts to build more permanent housing, the supply of new affordable units could not meet the demand.

At first, the Dinkins administration seemed to be making strides in housing families, in part because five-thousand units of Koch's 1986-1990 SIP housing program came on-line. As a result, the wait for permanent housing went from eighteen to twenty-four months in 1987 to only three to six months in 1990.[17]

Dinkins also made changes to the Emergency Assistance Rehousing Program (EARP) to speed up permanent placements. Begun in 1983, EARP pays stipends and bonuses to private landlords who house homeless families. For ten years, the program was generally ineffective until Dinkins enhanced it with supplemental federal Section 8 rental vouchers.[18] The vouchers helped families pay the difference between thirty percent (30%) of their income and the fair market rent. As part of this new EARP/Section 8 initiative, the city pays for a family's moving expenses, broker's fees, security deposits, and furniture, and landlords receive cash bonuses (see Figure 3.5).[19] As a result of Dinkins' changes, the number of families living in EARP apartments went from 721 in 1990 to

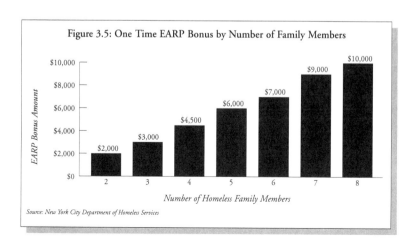

Figure 3.5: One Time EARP Bonus by Number of Family Members

Source: New York City Department of Homeless Services

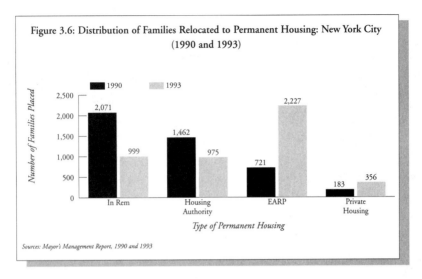

Figure 3.6: Distribution of Families Relocated to Permanent Housing: New York City (1990 and 1993)

Sources: Mayor's Management Report, 1990 and 1993

2,227 in 1993 (see Figure 3.6).

Although Dinkins' camp could point to the success of both SIP (Special Initiatives Program) and EARP (Emergency Assistance Rehousing Program), these programs could not keep pace with the growing number of homeless apartment seekers. EARP in particular faced the flourishing private rental market of the 1990s, which made many private landlords unwilling to participate in the program—no bonus could make it financially attractive to owners to pass up a private tenant who was willing and able to pay higher rent.

With these challenges, the administration faced a delicate balancing act between supplying enough housing and keeping more families from entering the system. By coming into the shelter system, a family was automatically prioritized on the city's subsidized housing list, displacing other poor but non-homeless individuals who might have been waiting for years for available slots.[20] But shelter providers who sought to place their clients in public housing projects were met with resistance by the city's Housing Authority (NYCHA), which was reluctant to receive "problem families" as tenants when there was a long waiting list of qualified, non-homeless persons. Finally, such homeless prioritizations were scaled back.

EMERGENCY ASSISTANCE: THE FEDERAL APPROACH

Throughout the 1980s and early 1990s, the homeless battle was not just being waged by the city, but by the federal government as well. The first large scale aid programs included the Department of Agriculture's Temporary Food Assistance Program, Health and Human Services' Emergency Assistance Program and Housing and Urban Development's Community Development Block Grants. In 1987, these efforts were overshadowed by the passage in Congress of the McKinney Assistance Act, the first, largest, and only major federal homeless funding initiative.

Originally called the Homeless Persons' Survival Act, the legislation was introduced in Congress in 1986 and contained emergency relief, preventive measures, and long-term solutions to homelessness. After the death of its chief sponsor, the act was renamed the Stewart B. McKinney Homeless Assistance Act and signed into law by President Reagan in 1987. Upon its enactment, the McKinney Act consisted of fifteen programs including emergency shelter, transitional housing, job training, primary health care, education, and some permanent housing. Just over $1 billion was initially authorized for 1987 and 1988, but a total of only $712 million was actually appropriated.[21]

In 1990, the McKinney Act was amended after Congress received new information showing that homeless children were encountering serious obstacles to their education. The new amendments detailed the obligation of states to provide access to public education to homeless children and youth, forcing them to revise policies that might act as a barrier to these children's academic success.[22] However, despite McKinney's significance, its programs have been hampered by insufficient funding. Critics also charge that the bill focuses too much on emergency measures, treating the symptoms of homelessness and ignoring root causes. For example, in 1993, seventy-eight percent (78%) of the funding was spent on food and shelter and only five percent (5%) was allocated towards education and job training (see Figure 3.7).

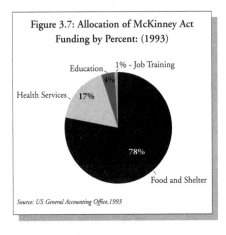

Figure 3.7: Allocation of McKinney Act Funding by Percent: (1993)

Source: US General Accounting Office, 1993

Nonetheless, the McKinney Act was, and remains, landmark legislation.[23]

NEW DIRECTIONS: TIGHTENING THE DOOR

In the rising tide of homelessness, everyone could agree that children were the main victims. Whether their parents were equally innocent was a matter of increasing debate. Some speculated that city policies had the effect of enticing not-yet-homeless "welfare queens" to join the shelter rolls.

There were also questions of eligibility, whether families truly needed shelter or were just unwilling to double-up, and whether the shelter system had just become a fast-track to an apartment. In addition, social workers were reporting educational, mental, and health problems among shelter residents that could hinder successful independent living. Coupled with this, public opinion of homeless adults was growing increasingly negative; they were widely perceived as drug addicts and alcoholics taking advantage of the system. It was a perception that reflected poorly on the entire homeless population.

In the decade to come, Mayor Guiliani and his administration would tackle these issues with a policy of "tightening the front door," screening homeless families more carefully to determine their true level of need. At the same time, sweeping policy changes on the national level ushered in an era of welfare reform, the consequences of which would have a significant impact on homelessness, and homeless families in particular.

NOTES

1. New York City Human Resources Administration, *Mayor's Management Report* (New York: New York City Human Resources Administration, 1998 and 1993).

2. Officials at the Emergency Assistance Unit dubbed Friday night "couples night" because so many couples would come to the intake center seeking shelter. These men and women would show up after-hours, when the EAU no longer had access to Tier II facilities, knowing instead they would be placed in a hotel. After spending the weekend in the hotel, many couples would disappear, only to return again the following week. Larry Schatt, personal interview, 8 Feb. 2002.

3. New York City Commission on the Homeless, *The Way Home: A New Direction in Social Policy* (New York: New York City Commission on the Homeless, 1992) 73.

4. Larry Schatt, personal interview.

5. *Mayor's Management Report, 1993,* 424.

6. New York City Commission on the Homeless, *The Way Home.* Commission Members: Mary Jo Bane, Alexander Cooper, Michael Dowling, Ronald Gault, Dr. Jerome Goldsmith, Victor A. Kovner, James Krauskopf, Victor Marrero, George McDonald, Felice Michetti, Verona Middleton-Jeter, Ralph Nunez, Larry S. Rhodes, Jack Rudin, Barbara Sabol, Jerry I. Speyer, Bishop Joseph Sullivan, Jane Velez, Nancy Wackstein, Frank Zarb, and John Zuccotti.

7. New York City Commission on the Homeless, *The Way*

Home, 13.

8. New York City Commission on the Homeless, *The Way Home,* 17.
9. New York City Human Resources Administration, *Mayor's Management Report 1993,* 402, 465-466. New York City Human Resources Administration, *Mayor's Management Report* (New York: New York City Human Resources Administration, 1994) 263.
10. New York City Commission on the Homeless, *The Way Home,* 72.
11. Ibid.
12. New York City Human Resources Administration, *Mayor's Management Report 1993,* 429.
13. New York City Commission on the Homeless, *The Way Home,* 72.
14. Manhattan Borough President's Task Force on Housing and Homeless Families. *A Shelter Is Not A Home* (New York: Manhattan Borough President's Task Force on Housing for Homeless Families, 1987) 122.
15. Tier II shelter regulations are encoded in the Part 900 Regulations of Title 18 of *New York State Codes, Rules and Regulations.*
16. New York City Department of Homeless Services, *Family Services Fact Sheet for Fiscal Year 2000.* Available at: <http://www.nyc.gov/html/dhs/fs-factsheets.html>.
17. Larry Schatt, personal interview.
18. Heather Haddon, "City Homeless Program Rewards Bad Landlords," *Norwood News* 4 Dec. 2002.
19. The EARP program is the city's largest re-housing program, and is administered by the Department of Homeless Services in conjunction with the New York City Housing Authority.
20. Larry Schatt, personal interview.
21. National Coalition for the Homeless, *National Coalition for*

the *Homeless Fact Sheet #18: The McKinney Act*, Apr. 1999. Available at: <http://nch.ari.net/mckinneyfacts.html>.

22. *Project Hope; History of the McKinney Act*, Available at: <http://www.wm.edu/education/HOPE/national/mckinney/mckinney.html>.

23. National Coalition for the Homeless, *National Coalition for the Homeless Fact Sheet #18.*

CHAPTER 4

THE MID 1990s
Getting Tough: A New Administration's Approach

The direction of homeless policy in the mid 1990s was shaped largely by the singular vision of Mayor Rudolph Giuliani, elected in 1994. At a time when the city was believed to be unmanageable and out of control, Giuliani sought to prove the opposite by prosecuting not only major, but even the most minor offenses. During his eight-year tenure, he pursued "quality of life" campaigns, one of which was to rid the city of the homeless by prosecuting squeegee car washers and subway panhandlers, under the theory that paying attention to minor petty offenses reduces all levels of crime and social problems.

The administration's drive for efficiency and order led to an overhaul in the delivery of welfare services, a cut in the city's housing development budget, and the transfer of many of the city's low-income housing units to private developers. Simultaneously, the depletion of affordable housing fueled the increase in the number of homeless families and would demonstrate that Giuliani's get-tough, regulatory approach to reform could not be so simply applied to homeless children and their parents.

NATIONAL CONTEXT

The economic and political tides affecting the nation provided the impetus for many of the homeless policy decisions made by city officials at this time. In the early 1990s, the country experienced a crippling eight-month recession, with the jobless rate reaching nearly eight percent (7.8%) nationwide, and eleven percent (11%) in New York City in 1992.¹ All told, 12.3 million workers lost their jobs between 1987 and 1991, and many of those jobs were permanent, long-term positions. When the recession ended, there was a lag before employment began to rise again, particularly in large urban areas like New York.

Despite the previous downturn, the United States emerged from the 1991 recession directly into an unprecedented ten-year economic boom. With the growth of the information technology sector and the proliferation of dot-com millionaires, many felt a new spirit of optimism, the sense that prosperity would triumph over poverty. In line with this thinking, the newly elected President Clinton campaigned on the promise to "end welfare as we know it." Like many policy-makers, he recognized that the decades-old AFDC (Aid for Families with Dependent Children) welfare program was in dire need of reform. Some states, including Wisconsin and New York, already had experimental programs to provide jobs to welfare recipients, which had been met with modest success.

The federal government was looking to expand such programs nationwide and a Republican-controlled Congress took President Clinton's pledge to "end welfare" to heart, drafting their "Contract with America," and The Personal Responsibility and Work Opportunity Act. Signed into law in 1996, the new law replaced AFDC with TANF (Temporary Assistance for Needy Families), ending a lifetime entitlement of aid, enacting new work requirements, and providing large block grants to the states with broad responsibilities for creating new work-fare programs.

Supporters of the law, including New York's Republican mayor, charged that AFDC created a class of habitual benefit abusers, encouraged fraud and laziness, and locked generations into a cycle of poverty. They cited the staggering number of welfare recipients as evidence: in 1995, one in every eight New Yorkers was receiving welfare benefits, 1.1 million people in New

York City alone.[2]

But the new bill was far more stringent than that which Clinton and his fellow Democrats had envisioned. It gave recipients a five-year lifetime limit to receive benefits, and a two-year deadline to find employment, although states were given flexibility to increase the lifetime limit at their own expense. In response, several states created their own welfare extension programs, including New York, which established the Safety Net Assistance Program because of the state constitutional requirement to provide for the needy.[3] Either way, the rules of the game had been changed.

CITY WELFARE REFORMS

The national legislation gave New York officials the mandate to develop new reform initiatives while tightening welfare eligibility rules. The state's two major welfare programs, AFDC and Home Relief, became Family Assistance and Safety Net Assistance. But the most sweeping changes came at the city level, where welfare programs are administered by local, rather than state agencies.

With the rules changing at the national and state levels, city leaders took the opportunity to overhaul services for the poor. Local officials were now following Mayor Giuliani's mandate: "the real meaning of compassion" is to help "people make the transition from dependency on government to a life of self sufficiency."[4] Operationally, this policy translated into more bureaucratic hurdles, including stricter rules and stiffer penalties, for those wishing to access services.

The Mayor's attempts to "close the front door" by creating hurdles to receiving government aid extended not only to homeless policies, but also to the city's entire approach to poverty and government assistance, in particular, the creation of two of the city's most controversial programs: the Job Centers and the Work Experience Program (WEP). The Job Centers are a revision of the city's welfare offices, or income maintenance centers, which traditionally administered benefits for clients. Though ostensibly in existence to help people find jobs, critics charge that Job Center visitors are frequently discouraged from applying for aid, and disqualified from employment programs. The Work Experience Program is likewise contentious, as it requires welfare recipients to participate in city work programs in exchange for benefits and at a quarter of regular union pay, making it impossible to earn a living wage.

However, despite these get-tough stances, the Giuliani administration did take a step forward on homelessness, making the Department of Homeless Services (DHS) a permanent agency. Prior to 1999, DHS existed on a trial basis under a "sunset" clause. With the passage of Local Law 19, DHS became a permanent independent mayoral agency on May 18, 1999.[5] For the first time, all services for homeless persons were consolidated under one authority.

THE NEW HOMELESS JOURNEY

At the same time that the Mayor restricted access to welfare benefits, he imposed a new hard line on the existing shelter system, creating a number of roadblocks for shelter seekers. To counter the perception that many families used the system to gain access to public housing, shelter entrance was restricted to only those who had exhausted all other alternatives. Special staff was assigned the task of investigating each family's housing history to help them identify other options, from staying with relatives to finding an appropriate apartment referral service. As a direct result, the number of families denied shelter rose from 365 in 1995 to 14,041 in 1998 (see Figure 4.1).[6]

With the hope of limiting family intake, the Giuliani administration attempted to literally close the doors to the city's Emergency Assistance Units (EAUs). The Human Resources

Administration had orig-
inally wanted to elimi-
nate the use of the three
EAUs in the outer bor-
oughs by establishing
one consolidated center
in Manhattan. But it was
the Department of
Homeless Services that
closed the Queens EAU
in November 1993 and
the Brooklyn EAU in
January 1994. Unable to

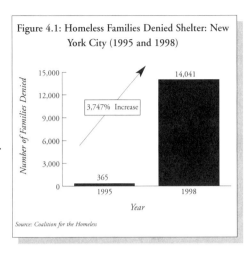

Figure 4.1: Homeless Families Denied Shelter: New York City (1995 and 1998)

Number of Families Denied

3,747% Increase

14,041

365

1995   1998

Year

Source: Coalition for the Homeless

find an appropriate site for the consolidated facility, they finally
closed the Manhattan EAU and extended the hours of the EAU in
the Bronx to around the clock. Still, the administration persisted,
seeking to eliminate the use of EAUs altogether by closing the one
remaining Bronx facility and instead referring families to the
Income Support Center or an after-hours hotline.[7]

Although the proposal was blocked by the courts, the administration remained convinced that "the existing shelter system has
sent the perverse message to those who are poorly housed, that it
is the only route to improve their living situations."[8] In turn, the
city considered offering various incentives to keep people from
entering the shelter system, from giving out bunk beds so that
families could better double up, to providing subsidies to families
opting to make their own living arrangements. Under these proposed reforms, families would still be allowed to remain in the
homeless housing queue, but not take up valuable shelter space.

ATTACKS ON LOW-INCOME HOUSING

As Giuliani worked on closing the door to welfare programs
and creating new hurdles in the shelter system, he also drastically

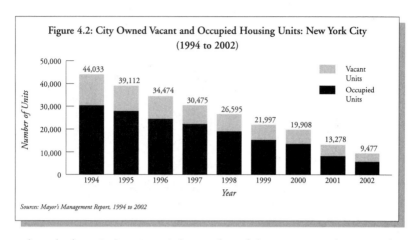

Figure 4.2: City Owned Vacant and Occupied Housing Units: New York City (1994 to 2002)

Sources: *Mayor's Management Report, 1994 to 2002*

reduced the city's potential supply of low-income housing by reforming the Department of Housing Preservation and Development (HPD). HPD had once overseen the transformation of city-owned, tax-foreclosed properties into affordable public housing stock, but now such properties were being rapidly sold into private ownership (see Figure 4.2). At the same time, an active campaign was underway to remove homeless squatters from abandoned city properties.

In 1995, Giuliani began the Building Blocks! initiative, a program designed to create low-income cooperatives by returning city-owned *in rem* properties to "responsible private owners:" landlords, private developers, non-profit groups, and tenant associations (see Figure 4.3).[9] Intended to stimulate community renewal, the initiative reduced city stock of *in rem* buildings to an all time low in 1999.[10] While the Building Blocks! program had good intentions, namely to create more community-based affordable housing, the city placed no requirements on what private owners could do with the property.[11] Some poor families watched as low-income apartments in their neighborhood were transformed into luxury housing, while others who had hoped for improvements upon local abandoned properties were left disappointed.

Meanwhile, similar threats were being posed to affordable housing on the national level. Nationwide, over 27,600 federal low-income housing units had been demolished by the end of 1999. Despite the Department of Housing and Urban Development's replacement goal of forty-five percent (45%), only 7,273 units, or twenty-six percent (26%), were

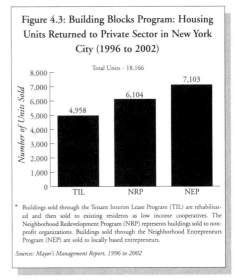

Figure 4.3: Building Blocks Program: Housing Units Returned to Private Sector in New York City (1996 to 2002)

* Buildings sold through the Tenant Interim Lease Program (TIL) are rehabilitated and then sold to existing residents as low income cooperatives. The Neighborhood Redevelopment Program (NRP) represents buildings sold to nonprofit organizations. Buildings sold through the Neighborhood Entrepreneurs Program (NEP) are sold to locally based entrepreneurs.

Sources: Mayor's Management Report, 1996 to 2002

replaced by the end of the year. Moreover, roughly 90,000 privately owned subsidized rental units were also lost, as landlords preferred to rent at market prices.[12]

Together, these events significantly reduced the supply of available affordable housing. And although supplemental programs such as EARP (Emergency Assistance Rehousing Program) and Section 8 helped to bolster the stock of subsidized housing within the City, its success was contingent on the willingness of landlords to accept Section 8 vouchers. In the end, many families, who often waited for upwards of eight years to receive a Section 8 subsidy, discovered that potential landlords found the private market more lucrative than subsidized program participation.

MORE CONTROVERSY

In the late 1990s, a series of well-publicized incidents involving mentally ill homeless adults inspired an even tougher city stance on the homeless. Although homeless families constitute a very different population than such high-profile miscreants as

Larry Hogue, the "wild man of 96th Street," and Paris Drake, the "Midtown brick thrower," the word homeless began to have a criminal connotation.[13]

In 1999, city officials responded by enforcing stricter shelter rules first issued by Mayor Giuliani and Governor George Pataki back in 1994. The regulations allowed homeless residents to be expelled from city shelters for a thirty-day period if they violated shelter rules, failed to comply with an assessment and a service plan, or failed to follow public assistance regulations. Mayor Giuliani took the debate a step further by proposing that all shelter residents be required to work or lose their shelter placement, and potentially their children to foster care. If a client refused to comply, they could be ejected from the shelter system. This in turn would put them in a position of not being able to provide for their child. With the child's well-being in question, the city could intervene yet again and place the child in foster care.

During the Mayor's brief senate run against Hillary Rodham Clinton, these shelter rules became a major campaign issue.[14] Rallies were held, petitions were signed, and Giuliani's opponent denounced the policy of allowing homeless parents to be separated from their children. Moreover, nearly all the city's non-profit operated Tier II shelters pledged not to cooperate with the new procedures. Ultimately, the courts found the new policies unlawful, since they violated the terms of rulings guaranteeing the right to shelter, including the 1981 Callahan decree and other subsequent decisions.

Still, the flack over the shelter regulations, workfare, and foster care marked a significant turning point in public opinion about homelessness. Media reports, combined with New Yorkers' personal experiences with the homeless in their neighborhoods, resulted in a collective realization that the city's quality-of-life campaign might be too aggressive in its prosecution of the homeless. New Yorkers may have viewed their neighborhood panhandler as a nuisance, but not as a felon and they could see how a revolving door between jail, shelters, and the street was not helping mentally ill homeless adults improve their situation. Still, Mayor Giuliani argued, "streets do not exist in civilized societies for the purpose of people sleeping there. Bedrooms are for sleeping."15

REFLECTIONS

No other New York City mayor incited more controversy for his stance on poverty and homelessness than Rudolph Giuliani. Towards the end of his mayoral reign, many predicted he would be most remembered as a crime-control tyrant, trampling on the rights of 23,000 homeless New Yorkers. However, the 9/11 World Trade Center tragedy changed that perception overnight. His actions in the wake of the attack were widely considered to be both compassionate and heroic. By the time he left office on January 1, 2002, mixed opinions had emerged about his pre-9/11 policies and their implications for his legacy.

On one hand, the Mayor garnered praise for his successful campaign against crime, a problem many were convinced no city government could solve. His proactive measures to combat disorder, fraud, and urban blight came in direct response to a groundswell of public opinion by city residents demanding a safer metropolis. Although some of his policies were extreme, Giuliani's supporters believed that it was part of the process of experimental new tactics.

On the other hand, 1993 to 2001 witnessed a retraction of many of the positive policy developments that had been made for homeless families. Even as the number of homeless continued to increase, Mayor Giuliani chose to ignore the rising tide of poor families, while calling for increased individual responsibility. Rather than garnering sympathy, homelessness became criminally suspect. But hard-line tactics, like the "street sweeps" to round up homeless men, ignored the circumstances of the larger number of homeless children and families caught up in the New York City shelter system. Their numbers continued to grow so that by the beginning of 2002, the typical homeless person in the city was a poor, minority child under the age of five.[16]

All told, the effects of the Giuliani administration's policy and national welfare reform forced New Yorkers of all political persuasions to re-examine which policy strategies might best help the homeless. As Mayor Giuliani left office, many expected his hand-picked successor, wealthy Republican Michael Bloomberg, to continue his predecessor's draconian policies towards the poor. Instead, the new mayor brought an unexpected commitment and focus to the issue.

NOTES

1. National Bureau of Economic Research, Bureau of Labor Statistics, New York State Department of Labor, 1992.
2. Mayor's Press Office, "Mayor Giuliani Opens Coney Island Job Center," *Press Release #239-01*, 5 Jul. 2001.
3. New York City Human Resources Administration, *Running Out of Time: The Impact of Federal Welfare Reform* (New York: Human Resources Administration), Jul. 2001.
4. Mayor's Press Office, *Mayor Giuliani Opens Coney Island Job Center*.
5. The New York City Department of Homeless Services, *About the Department*, Available at: <http://www.nyc.gov/html/dhs/html/aboutnycdhs.html>
6. Coalition for the Homeless, *Preserve the Right to Shelter: History*, Available at: <http://www.right2shelter.org/history.htm>.
7. New York City Human Resources Administration, *Mayor's Management Report* (New York: New York City Human Resources Administration, 1993) 403.

New York City Human Resources Administration, *Mayor's Management Report* (New York: New York City Human Resources Administration, 1994) 265.

8. New York City Department of Homeless Services, *Reforming New York City's System of Homeless Services* (New York: New York City Department of Homeless Services, 1994) 2.

9. New York City Department of Housing Preservation and Development, *HPD Announces New Round of Building Blocks!*, Available at: <http://www.nyc.gov./html/hpd/html/archive/rfq1-pr.html>.

10. Ibid.

11. Ta-Nehisi Coates, "Empty Promises: Housing Activists Say the City Wastes Its Vacant Lots," *The Village Voice* 12 Mar. 2003.

12. The Joint Center for Housing Studies, *The State of the Nation's Housing: 2000* (Cambridge: Harvard University, 2000).

13. Larry Hogue, a mentally unstable crack addict, terrorized East 96th Street in upper Manhattan during the early 1990s, vandalizing property and assaulting residents. He was in and out of jails and mental hospitals for years. Paris Drake, another mentally ill substance abuser with more than two dozen jail stints on his record, struck a young woman with a brick in 1999 near Grand Central Station. The incident received big headlines in the media.

14. "Homelessness Emerges as Campaign Issue for Clinton and Giuliani," *CNN,* 5 Dec. 1999. Available at: <http://www.cnn.com/>.

15. Elizabeth Bulmiller, "In Wake of Attack, Giuliani Cracks Down on Homeless," *New York Times* 20 Nov. 1999.

16. "Homeless Shelters in NY Filled to the Highest Level Since '80s," *New York Times* 17 Jan. 2002.

CHAPTER 5

THE LATE 1990s AND BEYOND
Conflict and Consensus

The beginning of the new millennium brought a renewed focus to an old problem. In 2002, in the wake of the World Trade Center disaster and the onset of an economic downturn, Michael Bloomberg was elected mayor and homelessness was once again thrust into the forefront. With an overall increase of twenty-five percent (25%) between 2001 and 2002 alone, the city experienced the largest one-year rise in homelessness since the modern shelter system began in the early 1980s.[1] The number of homeless families increased from a little over five-thousand in 2000 to over nine-thousand in 2003, with shelter stays averaging more than eleven months (see Figure 5.1).[2]

This influx of shelter seekers posed an enormous challenge to the new administration as they scrambled to meet the demand for

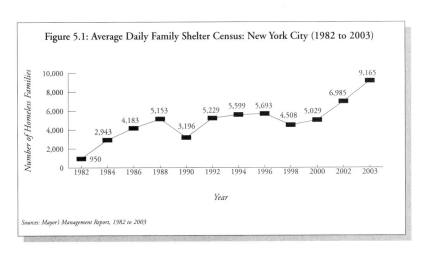

Figure 5.1: Average Daily Family Shelter Census: New York City (1982 to 2003)

Sources: Mayor's Management Report, 1982 to 2003

new beds. In violation of the court order prohibiting the practice of sleeping on the floor of the EAU, during the summer months of 2002, over fifty people per night did so; averaging thirty people throughout the year (see Figure 5.2).[3] In response, top Bloomberg aides converted the former Bronx House of Detention into a temporary family shelter. Partition walls were constructed and barred windows were concealed so that the gloomy space would be less foreboding.[4] But despite all efforts to make the old jail habitable, the move generated tremendous negative publicity for the city, from both advocates and the media alike.[5]

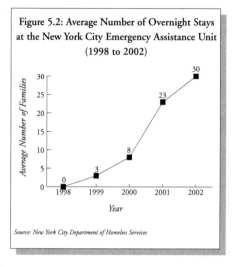

Figure 5.2: Average Number of Overnight Stays at the New York City Emergency Assistance Unit (1998 to 2002)

Source: New York City Department of Homeless Services

At the same time, a troubled sixteen-year-old boy committed suicide in a city welfare hotel. According to his family, he took his own life after the city threatened to return them to the EAU.[6] These two events created the impression that Mayor Bloomberg was not sympathetic to homeless families. After all, even conservative Giuliani considered, but ultimately abandoned, the idea of turning jails into shelters. And how could the EAU have deteriorated so much under Bloomberg that a teenager would take his life rather than visit there again?

In addition, the administration was criticized for its stance on who should be guaranteed shelter and who should be punished for disregarding shelter rules. For single adults, they proposed revoking the right to shelter for up to 180 days for failure to comply with shelter service plans. For families, they unveiled a

"Demonstration Project" permitting the city to place homeless children in foster care for thirty days if their parents turned down suitable apartments, arguing that some homeless parents repeatedly rejected worthy housing while holding onto much-needed bed space. Whether such punitive steps were necessary, as well as how the overburdened foster care system would handle the potential influx of homeless children, remains to be seen.

CHANGE FOR THE BETTER

Under Mayor Bloomberg, there were also some important and largely positive policy changes. In the winter of 2003, after twenty years of litigation with the Legal Aid Society, the city reached a historic legal settlement hailed as a victory for both homeless families and the city. It stipulated that policy decisions on the homeless would no longer be made in a court of law. Instead, an independent three-member "special master panel" would mediate disputes between the city, homeless families, and advocates.

In addition to oversight and mediation, the panel was created to review the city's current policies and develop a long-term plan. All parties easily agreed on the panelists: John D. Feerick, an experienced mediator and former dean of the Fordham School of Law; Daniel Kronenfeld, former director of the Henry Street Settlement with over thirty years of experience working with homeless families; and Gail B. Nayowith, executive director of the Citizens' Committee for Children of New York. The monumental settlement ended the ongoing legal battles that have shaped city policy toward the homeless for the last several decades. In 2005, the panel is scheduled to make policy recommendations and offer strategies for the settlement of all litigation.

Another commended initiative has been the administration's move to bolster permanent housing efforts through a more efficient use of subsidies. In addition to adding a new rental assistance program for those who have been in shelters for more than 730 days in the past four years, they expanded the Section 8 voucher program, from 2,700 vouchers in 2002 to a projected 6,000 in 2003.[7]

Even so, the city still has a way to go to fulfill its promise to effectively address homelessness, particularly regarding the permanent housing situation. The production of new affordable units in the city continues to decline. During the 1960s, 360,000 low-income housing units were built, as opposed to only 83,000 during the 1990s.[8] Furthermore, the units of affordable housing that are being built are targeted at middle-income working families. In 2003, the Department of Housing and Urban Development pledged $50 million for the creation of three-hundred units of affordable housing in lower Manhattan. But in order to be eligible a family must make between $50,000 and $85,000 a year, eliminating the segment of New York's population most in need of such housing.[9] Until this trend changes and more low-income housing is built, the burden will continue to fall on new shelters to compensate for the shortage.

Shelters: Yesterday and Today

For years, the city's shelters were viewed not as refuge places for families, but as destitute dwellings of last resort. In the early days, they were indeed stark, temporary, scary places. Families lived in gymnasiums, armories, and run-down hotels, and none were an appropriate place to call home. The good news is that most of today's family shelters are safe, clean, and private, with many featuring family living suites, common areas, and on-site social services. The bad news is that the process of obtaining a placement in this kind of Tier II shelter has become a long, difficult one.

The Long Journey

A family's trip through New York City's system of homeless services begins at the EAU on 151st street in the Bronx, where they apply and then await notification for eligibility for transitional housing, or at least a conditional shelter spot. While the entire facility is off-limits to members of the press and the public, some witnesses report that its chaotic atmosphere is reminiscent of an airplane terminal after a cancelled flight. Others compare the windowless, brightly lit space to a casino or an underground emergency room.[10] Since every family member must be at the EAU in order for their case to move forward, the space is congested with infants and children.

Since the Giuliani era, every EAU applicant has been required to undergo a protracted ten-day eligibility process to ensure that they have no other housing options. Applicants must provide a lengthy summary of their past housing situations and EAU staff call every family member and landlord listed to make sure that no one is willing to take them back. After this process, a little more than half of the applicants are found to be "eligible."[11] In theory, once a family is determined to be eligible, they receive a slot in a Tier II facility. In reality, due to the vast shortage of Tier II openings, many families are instead housed in inferior units intended for temporary, conditional stays with virtually no social or support services.

Something Old Is Something New

As the city looks for makeshift solutions to the modern homeless crisis, it is recycling old ideas. Officials have been weighing various options to reduce the almost $1 billion shelter burden.[12] Proposals that were received with fanfare in the 1980s and 1990s and later abandoned, such as housing families in mobile homes or congregate shelters, and putting EAU services in each borough, are again under discussion. In fact, the recent proposal to evict families from shelters if they reject a worthy apartment is remarkably similar to the much-debated suggestion from the Giuliani administration, to put homeless children in foster care if their parents refused to work.

Another recent proposal that harks back to an earlier era is housing families in retired cruise ships, docked at public piers. Putting indigent or mentally or physically ill individuals out to sea on islands or floating facilities has a long history in New York City. Fortunately, the idea was abandoned once officials realized the cost of refitting the ships would be too expensive.[13] Had it come into reality, turning cruise ships into housing could have led to more squalor and isolation for homeless families than the Midtown welfare hotels ever did.

Even welfare hotels, which once accounted for the majority of placements and later became near extinct, have recently reached nearly the same capacity as at their height in the 1980s. While most of the new hotels are no longer located prominently in Midtown Manhattan, they are part of a network of temporary lodgings to handle "overnight capacity" throughout the city. Some, such as the Hamilton Hotel in Harlem, are the very same ones that received such negative media and public attention nearly twenty years ago. After all the efforts to eliminate the use of such facilities, the city's payments to hotel owners has increased five fold in the last six years, to $180 million annually.[14] And just as before, residents report that the hotels are dirty, unsafe, and frequently the site of drug dealing and other illegal activity. Some even report that security guards routinely take bribes for larger rooms.[15]

Other temporary placements, such as scattered site housing, wherein private landlords enter into "arrangements" with the Department of Homeless Services, are also on the rise. Scattered site housing is one of the most expensive and least effective forms of temporary shelter, and yet its use is growing tremendously. In January 2001, just sixty-one families lived in scattered site units; two years later, the number had risen to over two-thousand, at a cost to the city of over $6 million a month, or $72 million a year.[16]

These units are of varying quality; some are poorly furnished, in dangerous neighborhoods, or in buildings that are not structurally sound. For this, landlords are paid up to $100 a night by the city, or $3000 a month, even though such units would typically rent for only a third as much on the open market.[17] Unlike Tier II shelters, which are less expensive to operate, scattered site apartments do not offer on-site day care facilities, employment training programs, or the comprehensive housing assistance that homeless families need. In scattered sites, it is landlords who are responsible for providing social workers, even though these landlords often lack the knowledge, expertise, and willingness to do so.[18]

Moreover, the introduction of scattered site housing has brought the shelter system full-circle. The city is once again putting homeless families in private, for-profit buildings, all at the public's expense. And again the city is paying for units in buildings with terrible health and housing code violations, with conditions completely unfit for small children. In one example, the owner of a building in Brooklyn owes $4.5 million dollars in back property taxes and has 640 housing code violations. Yet this same owner is currently collecting $5.8 million annually from the city to house 160 homeless families.[19]

It is hardly surprising that both scattered site housing and the city's use of welfare hotels have recently come under media scrutiny, prompting widespread criticism. Today, most of these arrangements are based on "gentlemen's agreements," hotel owners and scattered site landlords strike independent deals with the Department of Homeless Services (DHS), housing roughly five-thousand families without competitive bidding, contracts, or any public oversight.[20] The quality and location of most of these apartments and hotels means that many landlords can expect to earn significantly more money housing homeless families through DHS than they would on the open market. This, coupled with the absence of official contracts, has prompted some landlords to evict permanent tenants in order to replace them with homeless families. The Legal Aid Society has taken on the case of some of these evicted tenants, with one lawyer calling DHS "a remarkably lawless, almost rogue entity within city government."[21] Regardless of the outcome, the sad irony of the current situation is that many of these evicted residents will only end up at the EAU and enter the shelter system themselves.

At the beginning of the new millennium, the crisis of family homelessness is as bad as it has ever been. By the winter of 2004, the number of homeless families is projected to reach a record high of over ten-thousand. As the city struggles with an economic slump and high levels of unemployment, the Bloomberg administration is faced with housing more homeless families than ever before. How the administration will handle the growing issue remains to be seen; if anything they may be remembered for allowing the system to retrogress and expand beyond their control. Nonetheless, the first step towards a solution must involve a careful look at the root causes of family homelessness and, naturally, the characteristics of homeless parents and children themselves.

NOTES

1. Linda Gibbs, *City Council Testimony*, New York City Council Meeting, City Hall, New York, 18 Sept. 2002.
2. Ibid.
3. Ibid.
4. Michael Cooper, "Jail Reopens as a Shelter for Families," *New York Times* 12 Aug. 2002.

5. Jennifer Steinhauer, "A Jail Becomes a Shelter, and Maybe a Mayor's Albatross," *The New York Times* 13 Aug. 2002.

6. Nina Bernstein, "Mentally Ill Boy Kills Himself in Shelter Hotel," *New York Times* 8 Aug. 2002.

7. New York City Department of Homeless Services, *The Second Decade of Reform: A Strategic Plan for New York City's Homeless Services* (New York: New York City Department of Homeless Services, 2002) 29.
"Bloomberg Administration Seeks More Aggressive Plan for the Homeless," *Associated Press* 18 June 2002.

8. Steinhauer.

9. United States Department of Housing and Urban Development, *Martinez, Pataki and Bloomberg Announce $50 Million Affordable Housing Initiative in Lower Manhattan* (New York: HUD, 2003). Available at:
<http://www.hud.gov/news>

10. Jennifer Egan, "To Be Young and Homeless," *New York Times Magazine* 24 Mar. 2002.

11. Shelter providers are reporting that even young homeless children have been known to understand "eligible" in the context of shelter. These children might someday be applying for their own eligibility into the system, continuing the cycle of family homelessness. Some of their parents grew up in shelters, and a third generation of those who see shelter as home is not far behind.

12. Linda Gibbs, *City Council Testimony*.

13. Leslie Kaufman, "Manhattan: No Cruise Ships for Homeless," *The New York Times* 18 Jun. 2003.

14. Andrea Bernstein and Amy Eddings, "Handshake Hotels: Part 3; How a few big landlords benefit from NYC's homeless placement system," *Morning Edition*, WNYC, New York, 27 Jun. 2003.

15. Andrea Bernstein and Amy Eddings, "Handshake Hotels:

Part 1," *Morning Edition*, WNYC, New York, 25 Jun. 2003.

16. Nina Bernstein, "Many More Children Calling New York City Shelters Home," *New York Times* 13 Feb. 2001.
New York City Department of Homeless Services, Office of Policy and Planning, *Critical Activities Report, Family Services-Fiscal Year 2003* (New York: Department of Homeless Services, 2003) 2.

17. Nina Bernstein, "Many More Children Calling New York City Shelters Home."

18. Jill Grossman, "Shelter Skelter," *City Limits Magazine* Mar. 2002.

19. Tom Topousis, "They Owe, We Pay," *New York Post* 19 May 2003.

20. Tom Topousis, "Shellacked by Slumlords," *New York Post* 19 May 2003.

21. Tom Topousis, "They Owe, We Pay."

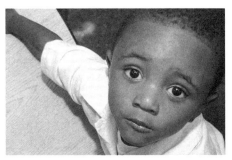

THE FACE OF FAMILY HOMELESSNESS:
Children are the fastest growing group of the homeless

TIER I • CONGREGATE EMERGENCY SHELTERS

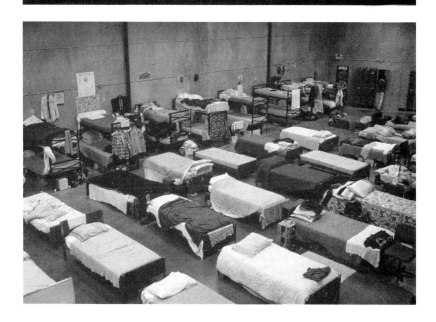

WELFARE HOTELS/MOTELS

MARTINIQUE HOTEL

SCATTERED SITE HOUSING

TIER II
TRANSITIONAL
HOUSING

N
E
W

C
O
M
M
U
N
I
T
I
E
S

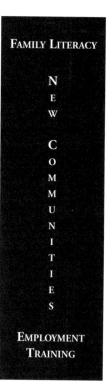

FAMILY LITERACY

N
E
W

C
O
M
M
U
N
I
T
I
E
S

EMPLOYMENT
TRAINING

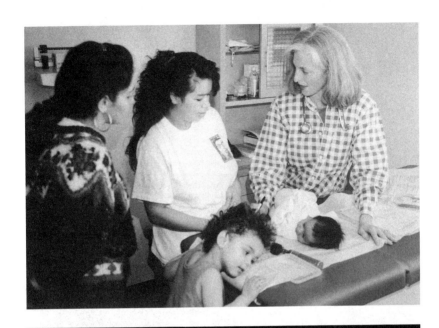

HEALTH SERVICES

NEW COMMUNITIES

GED / ALTERNATIVE SCHOOLING

CRISIS NURSERIES

N E W   C O M M U N I T I E S

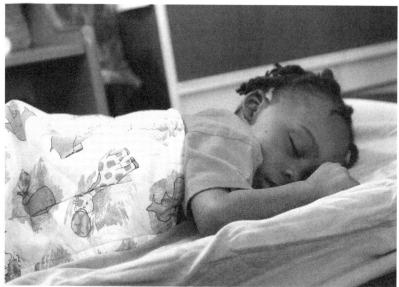

SARATOGA FAMILY INN • QUEENS, NEW YORK

NEW COMMUNITIES

SPRINGFIELD FAMILY INN • QUEENS, NEW YORK

CHAPTER 6

COMING HOME
The Reality of Housing Policy

As the homeless crisis worsens, the city continues to focus on providing immediate, emergency housing, sheltering families until they are able to leave the system. But what happens when they are ready to find a home of their own? The reality is that there is little affordable housing available. Efforts to achieve what seems like a relatively simple goal—renovating or building more affordable units—have exploded into a highly charged debate.

Much of the argument centers on whether to build permanent or transitional housing. Those who argue for more permanent housing believe that a massive investment in new affordable apartments is the only way to help families escape from poverty. While agreeing with the need for more affordable units, advocates for transitional shelter argue that a single-minded focus on building new housing neither addresses the depth of social service needs faced by homeless families, nor the complexity of the current housing situation and housing policy.

LOSING THE BATTLE: THE DECLINING HOUSING STOCK

While the need for affordable housing continues to grow, the nation's supply of units has been on a thirty-year downward spiral. The stock of such housing has declined so significantly that by 1995, the gap between low-income renters and low-cost rental units had widened to over 4.4 million.[1] In 1999, a landmark federal study revealed that from 1996 to 1998, the number of affordable units fell by nineteen percent (19%), or 1.3 million units.

This drop was largely due to the demolition of distressed properties and a shift of privately owned subsidized units to open rental market rates.[2]

Historically, low-income housing has been the domain of the federal government, but beginning with the Reagan

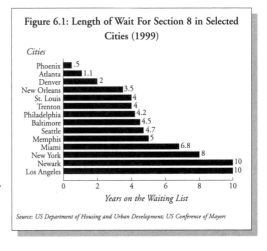

Figure 6.1: Length of Wait For Section 8 in Selected Cities (1999)

Cities

Phoenix .5
Atlanta 1.1
Denver 2
New Orleans 3.5
St. Louis 4
Trenton 4
Philadelphia 4.2
Baltimore 4.5
Seattle 4.7
Memphis 5
Miami 6.8
New York 8
Newark 10
Los Angeles 10

Years on the Waiting List

Source: US Department of Housing and Urban Development; US Conference of Mayors

administration, government essentially abandoned the subsidized housing business and the city has been unable to pick up the slack. By 1989, authorized federal outlays for housing assistance had fallen by seventy-six percent (76%), from $32.2 billion to $7.8 billion. One result of these cutbacks is extremely long waiting lists for government housing assistance such as Section 8 vouchers, and today there are over 280,000 applicants waiting for city housing services.[3] In New York City, these families will wait an average of eight years for a Section 8 voucher; in nearby Newark, New Jersey, the wait is ten years (see Figure 6.1).[4]

NEW YORK CITY: UNIQUE CHALLENGES

The challenge of keeping people affordably housed and out of homeless shelters is acutely felt in New York, a city where land is scarce and the real estate market is tight. Here the cost of rent is the highest in the country, with the market rate for a one bedroom apartment in Manhattan currently standing at $1973 a month, and $775, $723, and $568 per month for Queens, Brooklyn, and the Bronx respectively (see Table 6.1).[5] Between 2001 and 2002

Table 6.1: New York City Housing Characteristics
• Average Market Rate for a One Bedroom Apartment: 　　Manhattan　　$1,973/mo 　　Queens　　　$775/mo 　　Brooklyn　　$723/mo 　　Bronx　　　$568/mo
• New York City rents increased by 5% from 2000 to 2001
• Half a million New York City residents spend more than 50% of their income on rent
• The vacancy rate in New York City has never exceeded 4.01%.
• 2003 Vacancy Rate: 3%

alone, rents in the city increased five percent (5%).[6] Unlike the citizens of other large American cities, more New Yorkers rent than own, with half a million residents spending more than half their income on rent.[7] In a market where a five percent (5%) vacancy rate is considered normal turnover, low income rental units (those renting for $400 or less) had a mere one percent (1.26%) vacancy rate in 2002.[8]

Meanwhile, the income gap between the city's richest and poorest residents continues to grow. Between the late 1970s and the early 1990s, the average income of the bottom twenty percent (20%) of New York City households fell $794 or almost six percent (5.9%). Wealthier households fared far better, with the average income of the top twenty percent (20%) of households rising by $56,812, or fifty-four percent (54.1%). By the late 1990s, the average income of New York City's richest households (top fifth) was nearly thirteen times that of the city's poorest.[9]

In keeping with these trends, between 1996 and 1999, the number of low-rent units decreased while the number of high rent units increased. Vacant units with monthly rents of less than $400 (in April 1999 dollars) declined by sixty-seven percent (67%), and those renting for between $400 and $599 decreased by thirty-eight percent (38%) (see Figure 6.2).[10] These figures indicate a move towards gentrification, with formerly low rent enclaves, from Williamsburg, Brooklyn, to Harlem and the East Village to the Lower East Side of Manhattan, becoming the focus of high-rent construction and renovation.

As a result, some residents living on the fringe of the rental market can no longer afford the rent in the areas where they have always lived. Thousands of New Yorkers have been priced out of their own neighborhoods, making room for an influx of middle class newcomers willing to pay higher rents. Displaced low-income families must piece together temporary living situations, doubling

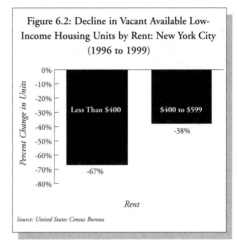

Figure 6.2: Decline in Vacant Available Low-Income Housing Units by Rent: New York City (1996 to 1999)

Source: United States Census Bureau

and tripling up with friends and relatives, before eventually turning to the city's emergency shelter system.

POSSIBLE SOLUTIONS: PROPOSALS FROM ADVOCATES

What are possible solutions to the city's deep-rooted housing problems? Housing advocates consistently call for increased rental subsidies, as well as for the creation of more housing linked with supportive services. Although both initiatives would be a step in the right direction, neither offers an all-encompassing solution, particularly in light of the scope of the issue and current financial and political realities.

Rental Subsidies

There is no question that families on the brink of homelessness would benefit from an increase in rental subsidies. Current subsidies for a New York City family of three on welfare stand at only $286 per month, less than one third of what is needed to rent a two bedroom apartment in the Bronx, let alone anywhere else.[11] In addition, poor families endure waits lasting years for Section 8 vouchers, only to discover that there is a severe shortage of private landlords participating in the program. Likewise, many families desperately search for Section 8 eligible housing, only to have their voucher expire before they find it. In 2001, one thousand Section 8 rental vouchers committed to homelessness went unused.[12]

Yet even if rent subsidies were to increase, ensuring that homeless families are given a better position in the rental market would be difficult at best. The market remains extremely competitive, and landlords and brokers know they can expect hefty fees and security deposits far exceeding those of EARP and Section 8 vouchers if they rent on the open market.[13]

Supportive Housing

Another initiative backed by housing advocates is more permanent supportive housing with attached social services. Many transitional Tier II shelters already use an approach similar to this model, providing families with extensive support services to prevent future bouts of homelessness. The supportive housing approach is different in that it requires a significant amount of upfront capital. Additionally, the level and amount of necessary services may be too extensive to be provided efficiently and successfully in an unstructured, permanent environment.

The up-front costs are perhaps the biggest drawback to supportive housing, which necessitates the creation of housing units where individuals and families could be placed. In 2002, a group of supportive housing advocates lobbied for a $1 billion budget allocation for the creation of just nine-thousand apartments with supportive services.[14] Unfortunately, nine-thousand units would not even be sufficient to house the city's current number of homeless families, let alone individuals.

Another concern is that there is not yet consensus among various stakeholders on what the idea of supportive housing means in practice. It has become a trendy initiative that does not seem to have been well thought-out. Some proponents advocate for permanent housing with off-site, community-based social services; others call for more temporary units with on-site services. Whether services are on- or off-site, and whether the apartments are permanent or temporary, makes an enormous difference in both the costs of supportive housing, and its effectiveness. Before New York could undertake such a project, advocates must come to a consensus on what exactly supportive housing would look like. Would families in need of services be mandated to seek them? Would there be penalties, or even evictions, if they refused? The state must also determine how much supervision and investment supportive housing would entail. Even with these critical elements addressed, the question would remain—how could the city assume the costs of creating the necessary units of affordable housing and the additional costs of providing expensive social services?

Nonetheless, advocates of supportive housing argue that although the approach would require millions of dollars of up-front capital, the city would ultimately save money since homelessness itself is so expensive. Arguing that when homeless people have problems, they use the highest-cost public systems, they claim that the alternatives are more expensive than the creation and maintenance of supportive units. Problematically, they frequently list the alternatives as jail cells, mental hospitals, or emergency room beds, spots that are certainly more expensive, but by no means the only alternative.

At a time of fiscal constraint, the city is hardly in a position to indulge in an initiative with such large up-front costs. It is simply not financially feasible, especially in light of the fact that a massive transitional housing system already exists in New York City. This system could fairly easily be transformed to provide all the necessary services described in a supportive housing model, but without the massive initial costs.

A New Dialogue: From Housing to Shelters

Any real and meaningful plan to end family homelessness must start with political honesty. As we have seen, the government has not, and in all likelihood cannot, produce low-income housing on any sufficient scale in the near future. Every night, thousands of New York City families with children call a shelter their home. From there, they commute to work and school, celebrate birthdays and holidays, and experience the joys and sorrows of childhood and parenthood. These families cannot afford to wait yet another decade or more until politics and finances align to allow for the construction of more low-income housing units. We must come to grips with reality: for the immediate and foreseeable future, we will have to work within the context of what currently exists. But in order to do so, we need to better understand today's homeless families and their immediate and long-term needs.

Issues like domestic violence, unemployment, and a lack of education weigh heavily here and may in fact be the reasons for their homelessness. Thus, the first step towards a solution must involve a careful look at the root causes of family homelessness and, naturally, the characteristics of homeless parents and children themselves.

NOTES

1. Jennifer Daskal, *In Search of Shelter: The Growing Shortage of Affordable Housing Units* (Washington, DC: Center for Budget and Policy Priorities, 1988).
2. U.S. Department of Housing and Urban Development, *Waiting In Vain: An Update on America's Housing Crisis* (Washington, DC: U.S. Department of Housing and Urban Development, 1999).
3. New York City Human Resources Administration, *Mayor's Management Report Preliminary Fiscal* (New York: New York City Human Resources Administration, 2003) 47.

4. Institute for Children and Poverty, *A Shelter is Not a Home— Or is it?* (New York: Institute for Children and Poverty. Apr. 2001).

5. NYC Rental Guidelines Board, *Affordable Housing: Where Can You Find the Lowest Rents?* Available at: <http://www,housingnyc.com/guide/location/html>.

6. Independent Budget Office, *Inside the Budget* (New York: Independent Budget Office, 12 Sept. 2002).

7. Nina Bernstein, "A Plan To End City Homelessness In Ten Years," *New York Times* 13 Jun. 2002.

8. New York City Department of Housing Preservation and Development, *2002 Housing and Vacancy Survey: Initial Findings* (New York: New York City Department of Housing, Preservation, and Development, 2002) 2.

9. Jody Wilgoren, "After Welfare, Working Poor Still Struggle, Report Finds," *New York Times* 25 Apr. 2002. Citing a study by the Center on Budget and Policy Priorities and the Economic Policy Institute.

10. New York City Department of Housing Preservation and Development, *1999 Housing and Vacancy Survey: Initial Findings,* 4.

11. "NYC's Homeless Lockjam," editorial, *New York Times* 14 Aug. 2002.

12. Linda Gibbs, *City Council Testimony,* New York City Council Meeting, City Hall, New York, 18 Sep. 2002.

13. In 2002, a landlord in the EARP program could receive a one-time bonus of $2,000 for renting to a homeless family of two, $3,000 for renting to a family of three, and $4,500 for renting to a family of four. Rental rates for these Section 8 apartments can be up to market rate, which is $845 for a studio, $940 for a one bedroom, and $1,069 for a two bedroom in 2002. For families, only parents with newborns can accept a studio, and only parents with a same-sex child are permit-

ted to move into one-bedroom apartments in the program. From Oct 2002 EARP Guidelines, Oct 2002. Available at: <http://www.nyc.gov/html/dhs/home.html>.

14. Elizabeth Olsson, "A Real Estate Bargain; a Push for Expanding Supportive Housing to Stem a Growing Homeless Crisis," *City Limits* Jul./Aug. 2002.

CHAPTER 7

A POVERTY OF ADULTS:
Homeless Parents Today

Twenty years ago, the typical homeless parent in New York City was a thirty-five year-old mother with a high school education and two adolescent children. She had probably worked at some point before becoming dependent on public assistance, and she was more likely to have been married to the father of her children than homeless mothers today. An overcrowded living situation, a personal crisis, an eviction, or a lack of housing options brought her to the EAU for temporary shelter placement in a welfare hotel, and eventually, permanent housing.

But today's homeless parent is most likely a twenty-seven year-old mother of two or three children, in all likelihood fathered by different men. Without a high school diploma, she has only worked for brief stints at minimum wage, and she now finds herself unemployed and on public assistance as the welfare time clock is running out (see Table 7.1). In many cases, her homeless journey began after fleeing a violent partner.[1] No longer does her arrival at the EAU signify the beginning of a journey from shelter to affordable housing, but rather, the start of a protracted battle just to be recog-

Table 7.1: Homeless Parent Profile: New York City (1987 and 2002)		
	1987	2002
Sex		
Female	92%	99%
Age		
< 25 yrs.	27%	42%
Marital Status		
Single	60%	98%
Education Level		
< High School	38%	55%
Foster Care As a Child	5%	30%
Employment		
Employed > 6 months	60%	10%
Employed > one year	36%	5%
Source: Institute for Children and Poverty		(N=408)

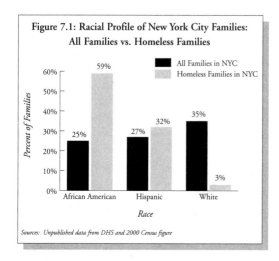

Figure 7.1: Racial Profile of New York City Families: All Families vs. Homeless Families

Sources: *Unpublished data from DHS and 2000 Census figure*

nized as "eligible" for shelter under current New York City regulations.

Today, a new generation of homeless parents has replaced the welfare hotel dwellers from the 1980s. They are significantly younger, more likely to be victims of domestic violence, and often foster care survivors. In New York City, fifty-nine percent (59%) of these homeless parents are black and thirty-two percent (32%) are Hispanic (see Figure 7.1). Ninety percent (90%) of them are single, female, heads-of-household, and two-thirds (66%) receive little or no support from absent fathers.[2]

Twenty years ago, being homeless was seen as a last resort for those living on the brink of poverty. Today, some homeless parents have found that instability and dependence are a way of life, so that coming to a shelter has been almost like coming home. Of the younger homeless parents, roughly ten percent (10%) spent part of their childhood in a shelter, and thirty percent (30%) were in foster care as children.[3] Fifty percent (50%) grew up in a family receiving public assistance, while the other half were children of the working poor.[4] There is even evidence to suggest that today's homeless crisis is a direct outgrowth of the mid-1980s homeless crisis. New York City homeless parents that are twenty-one years old or younger are three times as likely as those over twenty-one to have been homeless as a child.[5] But regardless of their previous experiences with the shelter system, today's homeless parents face a unique set of obstacles which must be identified in order to be properly addressed.

DOMESTIC VIOLENCE

Victims of domestic violence often live in transience and chaos: fleeing an abuser, doubling up with friends and relatives, staying at a domestic violence shelter, and often returning to the abuser once again. In fact, the average victim returns to her abuser six times before making a final break towards independence.[6] For poorer victims, this process is an even greater struggle, since many of these women lack the family support, financial assets, and community resources necessary for escaping violence. When their options run out, many find themselves homeless.

Today, domestic violence victims are one of the fastest growing groups of shelter seekers. A recent study revealed that forty-seven percent (47%) of all homeless parents have a history of domestic violence, and one in four of them cite such abuse as their primary reason for seeking shelter (see Figures 7.2 and 7.3).[7]

This legacy of violence is often passed on to the children of the victims. Thirty-one percent (31%) of homeless children have witnessed domestic violence, and observing such behavior in the home is a strong predictor of future victimization and abuse.[8] In fact, research shows that boys who witness violence by their fathers

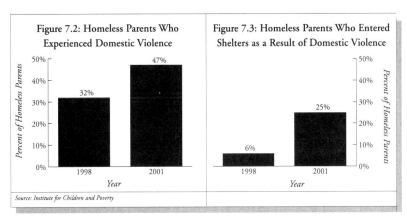

Figure 7.2: Homeless Parents Who Experienced Domestic Violence

Figure 7.3: Homeless Parents Who Entered Shelters as a Result of Domestic Violence

Source: Institute for Children and Poverty

have a one thousand percent (1000%) greater chance of someday becoming abusers themselves.[9]

In response, New York City launched a major media campaign in 2001 to promote a public hotline that victims fleeing violence could call. It was so successful that calls rose sixty percent (60%) from 1997. However, with bed space in domestic violence shelters expanding by only fourteen percent (14%) annually, the campaign has funneled the overflow of victims to the EAU and into the "mainstream" family shelter system. The situation grew so dire that the city's Human Resources Administration stepped in, requiring domestic violence agencies to take forty percent (40%) of their referrals directly from the EAU intake center.[10]

Nonetheless, the city's shelter system remains ill-equipped to care for the unique needs of these individuals. In particular, the system's scattered site housing (temporary lodging in isolated apartment units), is least suitable. This form of housing neglects the safety and emotional needs of a family by giving the apartment's landlord, rather than the city or a social service agency, the all-important task of providing social services. In most instances, the family's critical needs go unmet. In addition, there are serious security concerns for families with histories of domestic violence. Unlike Tier IIs, scattered site housing has virtually no security. Not only is there no one monitoring the doors, but scattered site buildings are frequently old and decrepit, often with substandard locks and windows.

FOSTER CARE

Many homeless parents also have a connection to the city's foster care system, some moving directly from foster care to homelessness. Thirty percent (30%) of homeless parents have spent part of their childhood in foster care, a fifty percent (50%) increase since 1993 (20% vs. 30%) (see Figure 7.4).[11]

Homeless parents with a history of foster care often have faced a different, more daunting set of obstacles. Forty-one percent (41%) were physically or sexually abused as children, as opposed to only thirteen percent (13%) of their non-foster care counterparts. Most had their first child when they were in their teens and became homeless at a significantly younger age (20 vs.

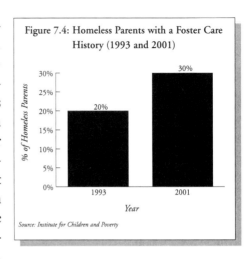

Figure 7.4: Homeless Parents with a Foster Care History (1993 and 2001)

Source: Institute for Children and Poverty

28). These women are twice as likely to become homeless more than once (47% vs. 24%) and many more become homeless as a direct result of violence (23% vs. 15%) (See Table 7.2).[12]

In contrast to the increase in homeless mothers with foster care histories, there has been a decrease in their own children's experiences with the foster care system. The number of homeless parents with a foster care history who currently have an open child welfare case has dropped considerably, from seventy-three percent (73%) in 1993 to only eighteen percent (18%) in 2002. Additionally, fewer of these parents have lost their own children to

Table 7.2: Comparison of Homeless Parents: With and Without a Foster Care History

Homeless Parents	Foster Care History	No Foster Care History
Physically or Sexually Abused as a Child	41%*	13%
Age First Homeless	20 years*	28 years
Homeless as a Result of Violence	23%*	15%
Homeless More Than Once	47%*	24%
Age First Gave Birth	19 years	20 years
Have Not Completed High School	59%	54%

*Significant at the .05 Level

Source: Institute for Children and Poverty   N = 446

foster care (30% vs. 17%).

There has also been a significant overall reduction in city foster care cases over the last ten years, which many advocates cite as progress on behalf of these young people. Yet few connect this drop in caseloads to the subsequent increase in shelter seekers. Between 1998 and 2003, the number of children in foster care in New York City declined by thirty-seven percent (37%), from over 40,000 children to 26,000. At the same time, the family shelter system increased by one hundred and seven percent (107%), from some 7,800 to over 16,000 children (see Figure 7.5).

The recent increase in the homeless family shelter census has been largely attributed to domestic violence, with twenty-five percent of women citing it as the direct cause of their homelessness.[13] This, coupled with the simultaneous decrease in homeless parents with open child welfare cases, may suggest that that the possibility of losing a child to foster care could be the impetus for a family to enter a homeless shelter. So many of these parents experienced foster care themselves, they may be more likely to leave a dangerous situation and prevent their own children from entering

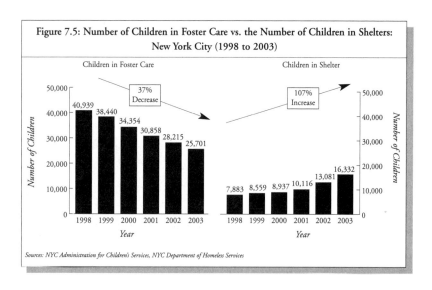

Figure 7.5: Number of Children in Foster Care vs. the Number of Children in Shelters: New York City (1998 to 2003)

Sources: NYC Administration for Children's Services, NYC Department of Homeless Services

the system. These trends may also indicate that the shelter system may be evolving into a form of family foster care, where rather than surrendering a child, a mother keeps her family together in a safe environment.[14]

TEENAGE PREGNANCY

While teenage pregnancy is on the decline nationwide, it is on the rise within the city's homeless population. Almost half of all homeless heads-of-households (47%) had their first child while a teenager (see Figure 7.6)—with the number of adolescent mothers in shelter jumping from thirty-seven

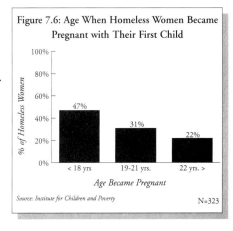

Figure 7.6: Age When Homeless Women Became Pregnant with Their First Child

Source: Institute for Children and Poverty   N=323

(37%) to forty-seven percent (47%) between 2001 and 2002.[15] These parents face many obstacles in life, including an incomplete education, dependence on public assistance, and a history of abuse. Coupled with homelessness, the challenges for these teen mothers become nearly insurmountable.

A recent study noted that over three-quarters (80%) of these young parents first had intercourse before age seventeen, and one-third (36%) by age fifteen (see

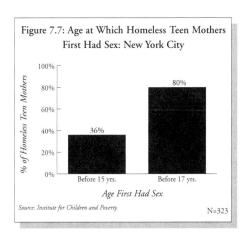

Figure 7.7: Age at Which Homeless Teen Mothers First Had Sex: New York City

Source: Institute for Children and Poverty   N=323

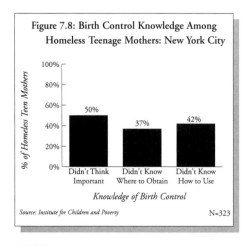

Figure 7.8: Birth Control Knowledge Among Homeless Teenage Mothers: New York City

% of Homeless Teen Mothers

Knowledge of Birth Control

Source: Institute for Children and Poverty   N=323

Figure 7.7). In sixty-five percent (65%) of these cases, a baby was born within one year of the onset of sexual activity.[16] Furthermore, most of these women are continuing a cycle of family poverty and teen pregnancy—fifty-three percent (53%) are themselves the products of adolescent childbearing.

These teenage mothers also demonstrate a profound lack of knowledge about birth control. One in two did not believe birth control was important, thirty-seven percent (37%) did not know how to obtain it, and forty-two percent (42%) did not know how to use it (see Figure 7.8). Equally disturbing, forty-one percent (41%) did not even know they were pregnant until the second trimester, missing a critical opportunity for pre-natal care.[17]

What's more, with the advent of welfare reform, these mothers face a disappearing safety net and fewer resources. Many of them have already experienced poverty and homelessness; thirty-two percent (32%) were homeless before the age of eighteen, and forty-two percent (42%) have been homeless more than once.18 With the added burden of early motherhood, it is difficult for these young women to obtain higher education, leading to greater financial stability.

JOB READINESS

In addition to facing domestic violence, foster care, and teen pregnancy issues, homeless mothers also have to find ways to support their families financially. These parents tend to fall into two categories: the unemployed—most of whom have never held a job, and the under-employed—those who piece together part-time employment with substandard pay.

Unemployed homeless parents face multiple barriers to finding work. Fewer than four in ten of them have ever held a job, therefore most lack basic knowledge of office protocol and etiquette.[19] The majority read at a sixth grade level, have never used a computer, and do not possess the reading, writing, and math skills required for many positions. Some have criminal records or substance abuse problems that make them less likely to be hired. The inherent difficulties of a life in poverty (including medical problems, transportation issues, and a lack of child care), coupled with the social stigma of being homeless, also reduces their appeal to potential employers.

Under-employed homeless parents, in contrast, have already overcome the initial challenge of finding work. However, they often hold part-time, short-term positions in the service sector and have not acquired the skills necessary to advance to positions with higher salaries, increased responsibilities, and job security. It is estimated that nineteen percent (19%) of homeless parents work; the majority earn minimum wage without benefits in places such as fast food outlets and retail stores.[20] Without a living wage and benefits, these parents are part of a growing group of working poor; working parents who, in increasing numbers, are unable to maintain a permanent home.

Compared to low-income parents who are not homeless, homeless parents are less likely to be employed and have had more disadvantages. While thirty percent (30%) of non-homeless welfare recipients grew up on public assistance, fifty percent (50%) of homeless parents have been dependent on welfare since childhood.[21] The average non-homeless public assistance recipient has worked for at least a year, and reads at a tenth grade level, while the typical homeless parent has a more erratic work history and reads at a sixth grade level. Sixty percent (60%) of low-income housed parents graduated from high school, as opposed to only thirty-seven percent (37%) of homeless parents nationwide (see Table 7.3).[22]

Table 7.3: Characteristics of Women Receiving Public Assistance and in Job Training Programs in New York City: Non-Homeless vs. Homeless		
Characteristic	Non-Homeless	Homeless
Average Age	29	22
Grew up on Public Assistance	30%	50%
Have a High School Diploma	60%	37%
Average Reading Level	10th grade	6th grade
Average Employment History	12 months	5 months

Source: Institute for Children and Poverty

Clearly, these parents lack basic education and skills to a far greater extent than their housed counterparts. This deficit makes it even more difficult for them to find employment that will pay enough to allow them to escape homelessness and stabilize their families. Furthermore, homeless parents are frequently ineligible for traditional job training programs, which require a minimum level of education and skills, often higher than they tend to have, putting them at an even further disadvantage (see Table 7.4).

Table 7.4: The Qualifications Needed for Public Assistance Recipients to Participate in a Typical Job Training Program vs. the Typical Female Homeless Head-of-Household	
The Typical Job Training Program Requires That The Candidate:	The Typical Female Homeless Head-of-Household:
• Be job-ready	• Has virtually no work experience
• Have a high school diploma	• Has a tenth grade education
• Read at an 8th grade level or better	• Reads at the 6th grade level
• Possess basic skills, such as typing	• Has few employable job skills
• Provide their own daycare	• Has limited access to daycare
• Have no substance abuse history	• Often has a substance abuse history
• Provide their own transportation	• Cannot afford transportation costs
• Have a permanent address	• Does not have a permanent address

Source: Institute for Children and Poverty

WELFARE REFORM

Ensuring that homeless parents have employable skills has become more crucial since the welfare reforms of 1996. The Personal Responsibility and Work Opportunity Reconciliation Act of the reform legislation was designed to put "work first" and eliminate life-long welfare dependency. Families can only receive federal Family Assistance (FA) benefits for a total of five years in their lifetime, and they are required to be working or in job training within two years of receiving aid.

In keeping with this new emphasis on work, New York City's welfare offices have been transformed into job centers, and eligible, unemployed adults are required to participate in the Work Experience Program (WEP), the country's largest public jobs program. WEP places participants in internships within city agencies, where workers receive below minimum wage rates for jobs that once paid a union salary. In addition to the issue of a living wage, "work-first" programs do not address the most basic needs of unemployed and under-employed homeless families: housing, education, and social support services. In practice, these programs actually run counter to the intentions of the welfare reform law, to lift families out of poverty and give them economic independence.

But the shift from welfare to workfare has had one intended effect: reducing the welfare rolls. The number of New Yorkers receiving public assistance declined dramatically. By 2003, the city's rolls were at their lowest level since 1995, dropping from more than 1.1 million to approximately 422,000 (see Figure 7.9).[23] Between 1993 and 2001, the number of rejected public assistance cases increased from slightly above twenty-six percent (26.5%) to forty-eight percent (48%) (see Table 7.5).[24]

Where do these families go when they

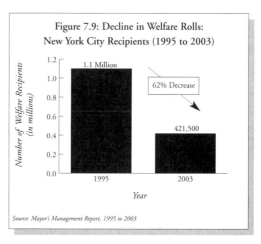

Figure 7.9: Decline in Welfare Rolls: New York City Recipients (1995 to 2003)

Source: Mayor's Management Report, 1995 to 2003

leave the welfare rolls? When the economy was growing in the late 1990s, former welfare recipients were more easily able to find full time jobs, even if barely at minimum wage.[25] With the recently stagnated economy, such employment has become more and more difficult to find.

Table 7.5: Public Assistance Applications and Rejections: New York City (1993 to 2002)		
Year	Public Assistance Applications	Applications Rejected	Percent Rejected
1993	264,900	70,199	27%
1994	262,200	71,581	27%
1995	277,600	120,201	43%
1996	216,600	120,863	56%
1997	212,200	115,649	55%
1998	200,200	113,313	57%
1999	197,200	101,952	52%
2000	203,200	84,328	42%
2001	186,800	89,664	48%
2002	192,400	NA	NA

Sources: Mayor's Management Report, 1993 to 2002

Moreover, the current economic shift from boom to bust occurs at the same time that many families are facing their lifetime limit for receiving public aid; therefore, the full impact of welfare reform in relationship to homelessness remains to be seen. But one preliminary study found that nationwide, thirty-seven percent (37%) of homeless families had their benefits cut and twenty percent (20%) became homeless as a direct result.[26] In San Diego, where roughly the same percentage of homeless families had their benefits reduced or suspended (36%), seventy-seven percent (77%) reported becoming homeless as a direct result.[27]

Even more disturbing, some families have had to give up a child as a direct result of welfare reductions. In San Diego, eighteen percent (18%) of homeless families who had their benefits cut lost a child to foster care; similarly, in Washington, DC, eleven percent (11%) had to place at least one child in limbo care.[28] And in New Jersey, ten percent (10%) of all those on public assistance who had their benefits cut gave up a child to limbo care as a direct result.[29]

WHAT CAN BE DONE

Insufficient education, domestic violence, foster care, teen pregnancy, unemployment, and welfare reform together place an overwhelming burden on a homeless family and the family shelter system in particular. As we have seen, these problems do not exist in isolation, but intersect in the web of family poverty. More and more, to be poor in this country frequently means that it is only a matter of time before becoming homeless.

As daunting as these problems are for these families, the scars may be more long-lasting for their children. Homelessness intrudes on every aspect of childhood, including education, health, and emotional well-being. Already we are seeing a second generation of the homeless; children who came of age in foster care or the shelter system of the 1980s and now are seeking shelter with children of their own. The best way to end this cycle is to focus on the needs of today's homeless children and recognize that homelessness has truly, sadly, become their issue.

NOTES

1. Institute for Children and Poverty, *Déjà Vu: Family Homelessness in New York City* (New York: Institute for Children and Poverty, 2001).

2. Institute for Children and Poverty, *Children Having Children: Teen Pregnancy and Homelessness in New York City* (New York: Institute for Children and Poverty, 2003).

3. Institute for Children and Poverty, unpublished data, 2003; Institute for Children and Poverty, *Hidden Migration: Why New York City Shelters Are Overflowing with Families* (New York: Institute for Children and Poverty, 2002).

4. Institute for Children and Poverty, *Job Readiness: Crossing the Threshold from Homelessness to Employment* (New York: Institute for Children and Poverty, 1994).

5. Institute for Children and Poverty, *Déjà Vu*.

6. New York State Department of Family Assistance, *Domestic Violence: Frequently Asked Questions on Reimbursement, General and Programmatic Issues* (New York: New York State

Department of Family Assistance, 30 Sep. 2002).

7. Institute for Children and Poverty, *Hidden Migration.*
8. Institute for Children and Poverty, *Déjà Vu.*
9. M. Kenning,, A. Merchant, and A. Tomkins, "Research on the Effects of Witnessing Parental Battering: Clinical and Legal Policy Implications," *Women Battering: Policy Responses* (Cincinatti, OH: Anderson, 1991) 238.
10. Tracie McMillan, "Sleep Disorder," *City Limits* 4 Jan. 2002.
11. Institute for Children and Poverty, *Hidden Migration.*
12. Ibid. A 1997 survey of 743 families residing in New York City shelters.
13. Ibid.
14. Ibid.
15. Institute for Children and Poverty, *Children Having Children.*
16. Ibid.
17. Ibid.
18. Ibid.
19. Institute for Children and Poverty, *Job Readiness.*
20. Institute for Children and Poverty, *Homeless In America: A Children's Story* (New York: Institute for Children and Poverty, 1999) 48.
21. Institute for Children and Poverty, *Job Readiness.*
22. Ibid.
23. New York City Human Resources Administration, *HRA Facts: January 2003*, Available at: <http://www.nyc.gov/html/hra/html.hrafacts.html/>.
24. New York City Human Resources Administration, *Mayor's Management Report* (New York: New York City Human Resources Administration, New York, 1993, 1994, 1995, 1996, 1997, 1998, 1999).
25. The Center for Budget and Policy Priorities reports that those who find jobs after welfare typically earn between $8,000-$10,000 annually, well below the $14,129 poverty line for a

family of three.

26. Institute for Children and Poverty, *Homeless In America*, 26.

27. Institute for Children and Poverty, *A Welfare Reform-Homelessness-Foster Care Connection?; The Story of "Lag Families" and "Limbo Children" in San Diego* (New York: Institute for Children and Poverty, 1999).

28. Ibid. "Limbo care" refers to a placement in either kinship care, foster care, or informally with friends.

29. Ibid.

CHAPTER 8

A POVERTY OF YOUTH:
Homeless Children Today

$\mathbf{F}$or most children, homelessness is not a brief or singular experience, but a period fraught with educational and emotional setbacks that can last for years. There are over sixteen thousand children currently in New York City's shelter system, and they constitute nearly forty-four percent (43.8%) of the entire homeless population.[1] These youngsters endure turbulent living situations, family violence, health problems, and instability in nearly every aspect of their lives.

EDUCATION

It is no surprise that homeless children struggle in school. In New York City, nearly a quarter (23%) of all homeless school-aged children repeat a grade, seventy-five percent (75%) perform below grade level in reading, and fifty-four percent (54%) perform below grade level in math.[2] Moreover, thirteen percent (13%) have been

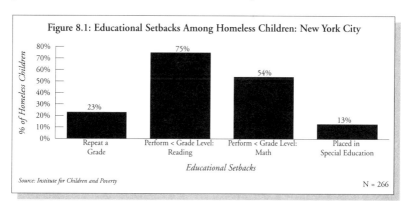

Figure 8.1: Educational Setbacks Among Homeless Children: New York City

Source: Institute for Children and Poverty

N = 266

placed in special education classes, a rate thirty-three percent (33%) higher than the average for school-aged children nationally (see Figure 8.1).[3]

ENROLLMENT, TRANSFERS, AND ABSENCES

ENROLLMENT, TRANSFERS, AND ABSENCES

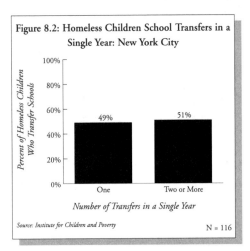

Figure 8.2: Homeless Children School Transfers in a Single Year: New York City

Percent of Homeless Children Who Transfer Schools

49%

51%

One

Two or More

Number of Transfers in a Single Year

Source: Institute for Children and Poverty

N = 116

Homeless children move sixteen times more often than the average American family, resulting in frequent school transfers, enrollment problems, and excessive absences.[4] Despite revisions to the McKinney-Vento Federal Homeless Assistance Act to address these issues, the problem remains. Although the new legislation allows students to remain in their home districts, transferring schools when entering shelter is all too common. In New York City, forty-nine percent (49%) of students transferred schools once within a single year, and fifty-one percent (51%) transferred twice or more (see Figure 8.2).[5]

The effects of such transfers can be long-lasting. Researchers estimate that it takes a child four to six months to recover academically from such moves.[6] In fact, homeless children who transfer schools are thirty-five percent (35%) more likely to have poor attendance records than those who did not transfer at all.[7] This can also stand in the way of special education placements—multiple moves leave little time for assessment, creating a double-edged sword for homeless children with special needs who are less likely to receive those services.

The McKinney-Vento amendment undoubtedly made positive strides for homeless children, not only by allowing them to stay in their school of origin, but also by requiring schools to enroll children even if they lack immunizations, prior school records, a permanent address or an accompanying adult. But there is a flip side to the legislation that is negatively affecting homeless children in urban areas. If children do not transfer, they often face arduous travel to and from their home district. A recent New York City study found that thirty-four percent (34%) of school-aged children spend one hour or more traveling to and from school, some trekking from southern Queens, near Kennedy airport, all the way to the upper Bronx or Harlem (see Figure 8.3 and 8.4).[8] Such long trips are not only taxing for children, some as young as first grade, but they are also spending valuable time on trains or buses when they could be attending after-school programs and getting help with their homework.

Ensuring that homeless children are actually attending school is another challenge. Regular school attendance is imperative for academic success, yet with frequent moves and frequent illnesses, forty-five percent (45%) of these children nationwide do not attend school regularly.[9] In New York City, thirty-seven percent (37%) miss at least two weeks of school per year, and thirty-three percent (33%) of these children miss more than one

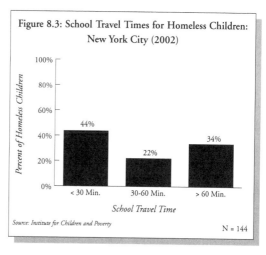

Figure 8.3: School Travel Times for Homeless Children: New York City (2002)

Percent of Homeless Children

School Travel Time

Source: Institute for Children and Poverty   N = 144

Figure 8.4: Schools Attended by Homeless Children Living at the Saratoga Family Inn:
New York City (2002)

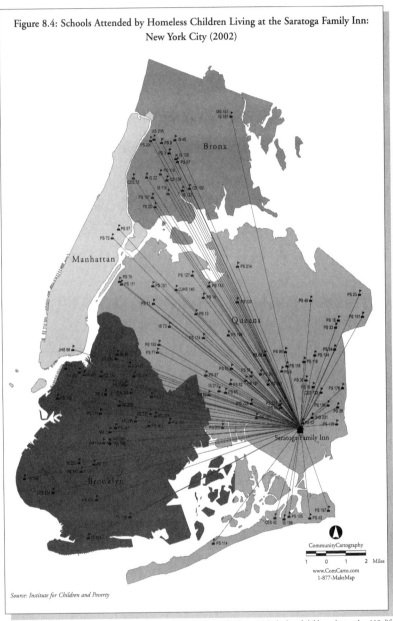

Source: Institute for Children and Poverty

The Saratoga Family Inn is a Tier II transitional housing facility in Queens that houses 226 school-aged children who travel to 110 different elementary and junior high schools throughout the five boroughs. Thirty-four percent (34%) of these children spend an hour or more each way traveling to and from school, causing them to miss valuable after-school activities and homework assistance.

month.[10] The impact of this can be devastating—two thirds of students who miss twenty or more school days in one year during first, second, or third grade eventually drop out.[11] That, coupled with the fact that in New York City, more than half of all homeless children are in grades 1-3 and experiencing chronic absenteeism, makes the likelihood of dropping out of school a real possibility for thousands of today's homeless children.

THE YOUNGEST LEARNERS

For the younger siblings of these school-age children, education is equally critical for their future success. Yet despite recent research demonstrating the importance of cognitive development during these formative years, the U.S. Department of Education estimates that only twenty-one percent (21%) of homeless children are enrolled in preschool programs, less than half the rate of all children nationally.[12] Without preschool, these children are missing a window of opportunity for early learning and the chance to offset developmental delays. As a result, the youngest of the homeless are three times as likely to manifest such delays as nonhomeless children (see Figure 8.5).[13]

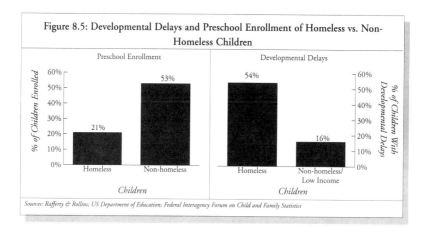

Figure 8.5: Developmental Delays and Preschool Enrollment of Homeless vs. Non-Homeless Children

Sources: *Rafferty & Rollins; US Department of Education; Federal Interagency Forum on Child and Family Statistics*

UNPREPARED PARENTS

Parents always play a pivotal role in promoting their children's education, but given homeless parents' own obstacles in life and educational hurdles, they often feel too unprepared and intimidated to become involved in their child's schooling. Forty nine percent (49%) have not completed high school, and the typical homeless parent reads at a sixth grade level.[14] The majority do not or cannot read daily to their child, nor are they able to provide effective assistance on school assignments. Without the guidance of their parents, children are more likely to fall behind: homeless children whose parents were not high school graduates are forty-seven percent (47%) more likely to repeat a grade and thirty-six percent (36%) more likely to be in special education classes than those whose parents did graduate.[15]

CHILDREN'S HEALTH

Irregular sleep schedules, inadequate shelter, constant relocations, and poor nutrition all take their toll on the physical and emotional health of a homeless child. In New York City, a midnight transfer from the intake center to a temporary shelter, followed by a six a.m. return to the EAU, not only exposes children to the elements, but it also makes it nearly impossible for them to get a good night's sleep.

These children also get sick at a rate that far outpaces other children of all income levels. Forty-six percent (46%) of the city's homeless children experience a decline in health after becoming homeless. They suffer three times as many gastrointestinal disorders, get diarrhea five times as often, fifty percent (50%) more ear infections, and twice as many hospitalizations as their non-homeless counterparts (see Table 8.1).[16]

Asthma appears to be one of the most enduring results of homelessness and the primary health problem these children face.

Across the country, twenty percent (20%) of all homeless children have asthma, almost three times the national average. In New York City, it is even more prevalent, affecting nearly forty percent (38%) of homeless children, more than four times the national

Table 8.1: Health Problems Among Homeless Children: New York City
Among homeless children:
• 20% have asthma
• 46% experience a decline in health with the onset of home lessness
Compared to non-homeless children, homeless children suffer:
• three times as many gastrointestinal disorders
• five times as many diarrhea infections
• 50% more ear infections
• twice as many hospitalizations
Source: Institute for Children and Poverty

rate.[17] These rates represent the highest prevalence of asthma ever reported in any child population.[18]

Since most homeless children lack a primary care physician, small, treatable, problems can easily spiral out of control. Ailments like ear infections, common to all small children, are more prevalent among homeless kids, and often go untreated, eventually resulting in permanent hearing impairment. Additionally, one report noted that more than sixty percent (60%) of two and three year old children in the New York shelter system had not been immunized against measles, mumps, and whooping cough, all preventable diseases.[19] Letting treatable illnesses go untreated is not only directly harmful to a child's health, but also impacts their school attendance, setting these children up for academic failure.

HOMELESS AND HUNGRY

In addition to other health problems, homelessness increases a child's chance of experiencing hunger. A poor or insufficient diet can be extremely harmful to children's emotional and physical well-being, as well as their future health, development, and academic achievement.[20] Nationwide, one out of every five homeless children (19%) does not eat enough, and almost half of those who eat less after becoming homeless show a decline in physical health.

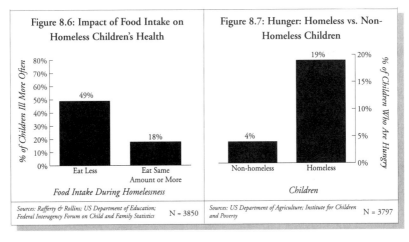

Figure 8.6: Impact of Food Intake on Homeless Children's Health

Figure 8.7: Hunger: Homeless vs. Non-Homeless Children

Sources: Rafferty & Rollins; US Department of Education; Federal Interagency Forum on Child and Family Statistics   N = 3850

Sources: US Department of Agriculture; Institute for Children and Poverty   N = 3797

In New York City, nearly one in four (23%) go hungry, a rate nearly six times that of non-homeless children (see Figures 8.6 and 8.7).[21] Ultimately, a lack of adequate nutrition increases the likelihood of educational and emotional set-backs, impacting their ability to develop into healthy, independent adults.

EMOTIONAL WELL-BEING

Nearly half of all school-age children, and one in four under the age of five, experience symptoms of depression, anxiety, or aggression after becoming homeless. In New York City these emotional problems are even more pronounced, with forty-one percent (41%) suffering emotionally after homelessness, and nineteen percent (19%) being taunted in school (see Figure 8.8).[22] Considering the chaotic nature of home-

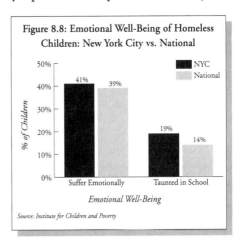

Figure 8.8: Emotional Well-Being of Homeless Children: New York City vs. National

Source: Institute for Children and Poverty

lessness, it's no wonder that these kids have emotional difficulties. But they also have to contend with being teased at school; homeless children often ride the "homeless bus" and when they get to school they are taunted, and told that their clothes smell like a shelter or that they have no home. Such negative emotions are dangerous; researchers report that suicidal tendencies are common among homeless children over the age of five.[23]

PUTTING IT TOGETHER: HEALTH AND SCHOOL PERFORMANCE

Whether children are sick, hungry, or depressed has a direct impact on their ability to concentrate and do well in school. Constant upheaval leads to more frequent illnesses and more school absences. And inadequate diets can jeopardize brain growth and cognitive development.[24]

Moreover, these problems can trigger one another—-hungry children are more likely to act out their aggression in the classroom, while asthmatic children are more likely to miss school, leading both groups to perform poorly academically. And the more often a child is homeless, the greater the risk for emotional and physical problems, as well as missed educational opportunities.

As devastating as these findings may be, many of the setbacks caused by homelessness may not be apparent for years to come. Children who fail to thrive at age three may be left back at age eight, and drop out of school completely by age sixteen. Every child requires stability and support to succeed in life, and homeless children are far less likely to receive either.

WHAT CAN BE DONE AND WHERE CAN WE DO IT?

New York City must explore how to best ensure that shelters are meeting the needs of children and their families. While there is perhaps no single cure-all for homelessness, steps can be taken so that the city's homeless system is better able to prevent and respond to poverty and a lack of housing. Only then can we ensure that the homeless children of today do not inherit a legacy of severe poverty and chronic homelessness tomorrow.

We have already seen how today's families entering the shelter system struggle more with domestic violence, lack of education, and unemployment than their counterparts of two decades ago. We have also seen how their housing options have dwindled away, as the government retreated from its commitment to low-income affordable housing. As the situation for families has changed, many shelters have also evolved, recognizing that programs and services must reflect the current reality.

Families are now staying longer in shelters, some for periods of up to two years or more. During this time, mothers can build their parenting skills or obtain their GED, and children can get after school tutoring and primary health services.

For the time being at least, shelters must be viewed as a new beginning rather than a last resort, and they must be made more responsive and pragmatic. The final chapter details a new vision for utilizing the powers of a shelter and transforming shelter institutions into true communities, communities of opportunity, within the larger community. Such a vision and transition is the only way New York City and the nation can begin to reduce family homelessness once and for all.

NOTES

1. New York City Department of Homeless Services, *Critical Activities Report-Fiscal Year 2003* (New York: New York City Department of Homeless Services, Jan. 2003).
2. Institute for Children and Poverty, *Miles to Go: The Flip Side of the McKinney-Vento Homeless Assistance Act* (New York: Institute for Children and Poverty, Jan. 2003).
3. Institute for Children and Poverty, *Homeless in America: A*

Children's Story (New York: Institute for Children and Poverty, 1999) 13.

4. Sheridan Bartlet, "The Significance of Relocation for Chronically Poor Families in the USA," *Environment and Urbanization* (9, 1) (1997): 122.

5. Institute for Children and Poverty, *Miles to Go.*

6. Laurene M. Heyback and Patricia Nix-Hodes, "Reducing Mobility: Good for Kids, Good for Schools," *The Beam: The Newsletter of the National Association for the Education of Homeless Children and Youth* (9, 1) (1999):5.

7. Institute for Children and Poverty, *Homeless in America,* 12.

8. Institute for Children and Poverty, *Miles to Go.*

9. Institute for Children and Poverty, *Homeless in America,* 13.

10. Institute for Children and Poverty, *Miles to Go.*

11. Heyback and Nix-Hodes, 5.

12. Institute for Children and Poverty, *Homeless in America,* 11.

13. Yvonne Rafferty and Norma Rollins, *Learning in Limbo: The Educational Deprivation of Young Homeless Children* (New York: Advocates for Children of New York, Inc., 1989) 39.

14. Ibid.

15. Institute for Children and Poverty, *Homeless in America,* 14.

16. Meagan Sandel, Joshua Sharfstein, and Randy Shaw, *There's No Place Like Home: How America's Housing Crisis Threatens Our Children* (San Francisco: Housing America, 1999) 8-9.

17. Bob Herbert, "In America; Children in Crisis," *New York Times* 10 Jun. 1999. See also: "Still in Crisis: The Health Status of New York's Homeless Children," a publication of the Children's Health Fund.

18. Herbert, "In America; Children in Crisis."

19. Ibid.

20. Second Harvest, *Who We Serve/Hunger: The Faces & Facts, Health and Social Consequences* (Chicago: Second Harvest, 1999).

21. Institute for Children and Poverty, *Homeless in America*, 21.
22. Institute for Children and Poverty, *Homeless in America*, 17.
23. Mark Rosenman and Mary Lee Stein, "Homeless Children: A New Vulnerability," *Homeless Children: The Watchers and Waiters* (Binghamton: Haworth Press, 1990) 95.
24. Irwin Redlener, *Still In Crisis: The Health Status of New York's Homeless Children* (New York: Children's Defense Fund, 1999).

CHAPTER 9

NEW COMMUNITIES OF OPPORTUNITY

Tonight almost half a million families with over one million children will be homeless in America. We have seen how officials in one city responded to this crisis, trying one makeshift solution after another, from emergency assistance units to congregate shelters, from welfare hotels to scattered site housing. And yet these measures only address one aspect of homelessness—a lack of housing—and not its root causes. As a result, the number of homeless families continues to grow, shelters remain at capacity, and new facilities open regularly.

Twenty years ago, city shelters were no place for any family to call home. Their basic mission was simply emergency housing and little more. As a result, families remained entrenched in poverty, and many became homeless a second, third, or even fourth time. New York City's recidivism rate was a full fifty percent (50%), and many of today's shelter residents themselves came of age within the emergency shelters that defined the period.[1]

Two decades later, shelters are still here, but many have evolved into very different places—dynamic, multi-service centers addressing the comprehensive needs of homeless families. With very little affordable housing being built, shelters have become one of the only housing options low-income families have. In fact, they may be the twenty-first century's version of affordable housing.

As we attempt to end the cycle of family homelessness, the answer may lie in these facilities of the new millennium, shelters turned into "communities of opportunity." Shelters have become powerful places where enormous changes in people's lives and habits are taking place. They either are, or can be, residential educational training centers where families live and participate in programs addressing the root causes of poverty. In fact, today these facilities are at the forefront of the war on poverty, fighting domestic violence, teen pregnancy, illiteracy, illness, and foster care placements, while simultaneously providing job readiness, employment training, and education, all on-site.

Indeed, shelters have become the new "main streets" of poor communities, serving as an alternative approach to providing community services in a residential setting under one roof. And why not? If shelters have become more permanent than ever before, and in many ways are taking the place of old, newly gentrified neighborhoods, then their power should be harnessed and their potential to transform people's lives recognized.

Some argue that this view of a shelter is misguided, acting as a barrier to the construction of permanent housing, but we must ask the fundamental question: when will this housing be built? Whether intentional or not, government has essentially abandoned its commitment to low-income housing. Today when government speaks of affordable housing, the question remains— affordable for whom? New York City's new initiative to develop three-hundred units of affordable housing in downtown Manhattan is a perfect example. Qualifying applicants must earn between $50,000 and $85,000 annually. No low-income families meet that criteria, and homeless families never will. For the time being, shelters are all that is left. They have become surrogate low-income housing where poor families presently reside and will probably continue to do so for the foreseeable future. And, if, as we have seen, homelessness is more complex than just housing, shelter communities can play a highly significant role in reducing homelessness itself.

SHELTERS AND LEARNING

A lack of education lies at the heart of today's poverty problems. Nearly one-half of homeless parents have not completed high school, limiting not only their own potential, but also rendering them less able to promote their children's educational development.

An investment in homeless parents is also an investment in homeless children, and shelter communities are places where parents have a chance to connect with their children in ways they may never have before. Parenting classes, parent-child activities, and on-site childcare are among the programs giving parents insight into their children's emotional, physical, and intellectual development, and helping them become more active and engaged mothers and fathers. Parent-child literacy programs, like the "Together In Learning" model piloted in several New York shelters and shelters in fifteen other cities nationwide, enable parents to further their own literacy level while engaging in games, stories, and literacy projects with their children.[2] For the first time, young homeless parents are gaining the skills to become their children's first teachers, and later, to become advocates in their classrooms. With nearly half of the nation lacking the basic reading skills necessary to function in our society, shelters can become important frontline vehicles for supporting literacy efforts.[3]

At the same time as parents are making these crucial educational strides, we can ensure that their children do the same. If we are to prevent yet another generation of children from becoming homeless parents themselves, we must recognize the issues they face and address them early and comprehensively. As we have seen, homeless children have profound educational, health, and emotional needs that must be met through early intervention and ongoing educational support. With shelter stays getting longer for families, homeless children have come to know a shelter as their "home," and it is in this "home" that they receive support, encouragement, and guidance as they embark on their educational journey.

In New York City, over half of all homeless children change schools at least once a year, resulting in months of academic setbacks. They miss weeks of classes because of homelessness and are held back and wrongfully placed in remedial programs. Moreover, many of them spend over an hour traveling to and from school, and many are regularly taunted for being homeless by their classmates. These are hardly the ingredients for academic success.

But there is proof that focusing on the needs of these children results in remarkable academic, social, and emotional gains. A recent study of a New York City shelter-based after-school program found that children made significant academic gains in as little as six months, with fifty-nine percent improving their overall grade point average and sixty percent and fifty-six percent showing increases in their reading and math scores respectively (see Figure 9.1).[4] Not only do their grades improve, so does their self-confidence and behavior; over three quarters of these children feel better about their own abilities since attending the program and eighty-three percent are more cooperative.[5]

Furthermore, shelter-based educational enrichment activities have a positive impact on school attendance and parental involvement. One study found that ninety-two percent of homeless children in after-school programs have a high rate of daily school attendance, compared to only sixty-three percent of those not attending such programs. In addition, these programs have proved beneficial in helping homeless parents form partnerships with their children's schools—almost all of those with children enrolled in these programs visit their children's schools frequently, while only a quarter of those with children not attending do the same.[6]

For younger children, pre-school programs in shelter communities have had an enormous impact on their social, emotional,

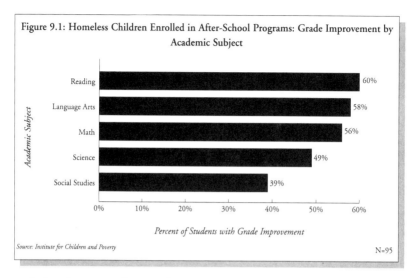

Figure 9.1: Homeless Children Enrolled in After-School Programs: Grade Improvement by Academic Subject

Source: Institute for Children and Poverty   N=95

and developmental growth. In as little as eight weeks, homeless children attending pre-school have demonstrated dramatically improved language skills, longer attention spans, more cooperative behavior, and greater self-confidence.[7] While it is widely acknowledged that pre-school programs are an important precursor for academic success, for many of these children, this is the first time they have had access to it, which is more readily available to them in a shelter community than in their old neighborhoods.

SHELTERS AND EMPLOYMENT

With few homeless parents having ever held a job, and fewer still having graduated from high school, we must initiate educational programs within shelters and teach the writing and math skills necessary for success in the workplace.[8]

Shelters should include education and GED preparation, mentoring and skill building, and job internships and actual employment, both on-site and in the community. For underemployed parents, who usually have held only brief, part-time positions, the emphasis is on gaining the skills to embark on a more viable career path. For those with work experience, the emphasis is on job retention and advancement. Shelters can become the equivalent of a school campus, where some parents "major" in computers, while others prepare to become home day care providers; where some are trained as security officers, and others become teacher's aides or maintenance workers. The possibilities are endless.

If the goal is to move people from public assistance to work and to end homelessness, then we must provide the tools to make it happen. And in a shelter-turned-community we can begin this process. It is time to take seriously the opportunity to deal with the poverty problems homeless families currently face and to do so where they currently live, in the shelter communities that exist within larger communities.

SHELTERS AND FOSTER CARE

With a third of today's shelter residents having spent some part of their childhood in foster care and many moving directly from the foster care system into the shelter system, there is an immediate need to prevent their children from doing the same.[9]

One approach is shelter crisis nurseries, which provide twenty-four-hour, seven day a week temporary placements for children at risk of abuse or neglect. Parents deal with emergencies and sort out stressful situations that put their child at risk, and a whole new way of handling crises is learned. Through after-care and support services, crisis nursery staff work with each family to ensure their long-term stability, keeping families together in a safe and nurturing environment. In the end, it is not just the children and their families who benefit, but the public as well: a foster care placement can cost up to $40,000 per child annually, while the annual cost of the shelters' crisis service is approximately $750 per child.[10] Shelter crisis nurseries can offer powerful alternatives, and within the larger network of services available in the shelter-turned-community, they can prevent a lifetime of dependency within the foster care system.

SHELTERS AND TEEN PREGNANCY

Many homeless heads-of-household had their first child while still a teenager and more than half are themselves the products of adolescent childbearing.[11] Most of these young mothers may lack the maturity and the skills to make good parenting decisions and manage their lives. For this group, most of whom dropped out of high school, educational programs can help establish goals and direction, while allowing them to gain a sense of their own potential—natural incentives to family planning and the postponement of future childbearing. They can attend GED classes to complete their schooling as well as job readiness, employment training, and parenting skills workshops. They can learn that education and work are important precursors to having children, successfully raising a family, and ensuring that their children have a solid foundation for the future. And they can begin to do this all within the residential educational environment of a shelter-turned-community.

SHELTERS AND DOMESTIC VIOLENCE

Almost half of all homeless parents have a history of domestic violence, and nearly a third of homeless children have witnessed it. Boys who do so have a one thousand percent greater chance of becoming abusers themselves.[12] In fact, many homeless families cite domestic violence as their primary reason for becoming homeless.

With these victims entering the shelter system at increasing rates, there is an immediate opportunity to tackle this problem in a safe and nurturing environment. A mother can access supportive services to address both her physical and emotional health within the stable, safe shelter environment. Her children can have the opportunity to address the emotional ramifications of living in an abusive household; educational, social programs provide the support they need to fully recover.

SHELTERS AND CHILDREN'S HEALTH

Homeless children are sick more frequently and have significantly higher rates of hunger than their non-homeless counterparts. In New York City, almost three-quarters of all homeless families have no primary care physician, instead utilizing emergency rooms and walk-in clinics for their medical care.[13]

Shelters should, and many do, have on-site medical services, nutrition classes, and exercise programs. They connect parents and children to services in area hospitals. For those services not available on-site, shelters could partner with local health providers and other community organizations. For the first time, these families have access to the primary care services that are critical for staying healthy, as well as gain resources that promote a healthy lifestyle.

SHELTERS AND COMMUNITY

Part of the power of a shelter-turned-community is the potential for positive collaborations with the larger community. Local libraries, community colleges, museums, and cultural institutions can help enhance a shelter's services and provide extracurricular activities. Children can be connected to mentors at a high school, receive one-on-one academic assistance at a library, and find a place in the spotlight in a local theater troupe. Adults can be linked to employment opportunities with community businesses and take their first steps on the road to independent living. In fact, New York City is rich with access to such opportunities; and with a shelter recognized as a new community within the larger community, all kinds of needs can be met.

Shelters are much more than just temporary housing for the poor. Many have become visionary residential community centers handling front-line poverty and dealing it a powerful blow. These new communities, partnering with the broader community, offer enormous benefits to those in need, and they do so at a reasonable cost. In New York City, the estimated cost of a shelter-turned-community is roughly $25 per person per day, including housing, education, childcare, and a full spectrum of programs and activities.[14]

In addition to cost, these communities offer families a safer, more respectable living environment than the congregate emergency shelters that preceded them. With private living suites, indoor and outdoor play areas, computer labs, and classrooms; the atmosphere is one of a community center rather than a stark city shelter. These residences are essentially "one stop shops," where all the programs and services a family needs to move forward are found under one roof.

Furthermore, this on-site approach, coupled with positive peer pressure from shelter residents and counselors, removes many of the traditional obstacles to program participation. The logistical nightmares of attempting to participate in educational and social programs, historically spread throughout the community, are gone. The search for transportation and childcare no longer stands in the way. Parents and children simply have to walk down the hall or go up the stairs to participate in services that will change their lives. Such is the power of a shelter community.

This is an approach already proven successful. In New York City, many Tier II facilities are working to address poverty and homelessness in new and dynamic ways. Shelters have transformed into communities of opportunity, where shelter directors advocate for resources for their residents just as elected officials do for their constituents, and staff members link families to a variety of education and employment options just like guidance counselors do for their students.

Simply put, turning shelters into communities of opportunity is an approach that works. It is truly the first step to ending family homelessness as we have known it. Families who partake in the power of a shelter are able to overcome their homelessness, move into new homes, and stay housed. Studies have shown that after two years, ninety percent of program participants in such communities maintained their permanent housing.[15] Already, thousands of families who have come through these new communities have found housing and secure jobs, while furthering their education and strengthening their families. They have emerged from homelessness largely because of a common sense approach that takes a negative circumstance and transforms it into a positive opportunity for success.

A city government, which for so long has tried to curtail and deal with the growth of family homelessness, has unexpectedly laid the groundwork to effectively reduce it permanently. The Tier II shelter system in New York City is a national model for effectively managing homelessness. The only drawback is that few people readily recognize it for what it truly is—one of the most ambitious and comprehensive anti-poverty programs ever launched by a local municipality. These facilities have harnessed all of the previously dispersed community-based services and redeployed them in new, innovative, cost-effective ways, within new temporary communities. But they are temporary in that they are only the first step. The steps in this transition are similar to those all young people take after graduating from school. They move away from home, become independent, get their first job, and rent their first apartment. At the beginning, their living arrangements and their jobs may not be ideal; however, as they develop more skills and obtain more education, they are better able to move up and out of one community into another.

In the early 1980s, the Reagan administration set all this in motion when they began eliminating funding for low-income housing. The dissipation of this funding ensured that court-mandated integrated housing for the poor would be kept away from urban and suburban middle-class neighborhoods. If you don't have the money, you can't build the housing. From that day forward it was clear that it was only a matter of time before the poor were living in places other than traditional low-income housing; today's family shelter system was born. Shelters became the supposed temporary alternative, springing up in dilapidated industrial or residential areas. But twenty years later, they are both more permanent and more numerous than ever. Still, it would not be until the Clinton presidency and the tenure of HUD Secretary Cuomo that the Federal government would play an active role in enhancing shelters and their services by supporting transitional housing and the funding of a complete continuum of care. More services were added to make shelters more humane, and the whole nature of a shelter began to change.

Today, there is a new response to homelessness—a Ten-Year Plan coming out of Washington, DC. It purports to end homelessness by closing the so-called "front door." By closing shelters and dismantling programs, the plan expects the homeless to be absorbed into other existing service systems. It is in fact, reminiscent of the 1980's "just say no" anti-drug and teen pregnancy campaigns, illogical approaches that do nothing about a problem except expect it to disappear. The Ten-Year Plan is already several years old and little has changed; the homeless keep coming, and only lip service is paid to the development of new low-income housing. If the truth be told, without a massive, immediate infusion of affordable housing for the poor, no plan, regardless of its timetable, can succeed. And with the national government functioning in a quasi-war economy and national and local deficits estimated to be in the trillions of dollars, it is inconceivable that any such initiative will be taken. In reality, the Ten-Year Plan is already dated, and represents an abdication of responsibility rather than a viable solution to the multi-faceted problem of homelessness.

Instead, those truly concerned with ending family homelessness are at a crossroads. They could, and should, continue to advocate for new housing, understanding that it still remains a long-term goal. They could also abandon viable solutions, and buy into the national ten-year plan, discovering several years from now that they have helped to usher in a new generation of the homeless. Or they could recognize the true breadth and depth of the problem, work within the environment and infrastructure already in place, and deal a powerful blow against family homelessness and severe poverty.

This book has described the history and reality of family homelessness in New York City, but the problems and solutions are similar everywhere, only the magnitude of the problem differs. New York has inadvertently developed a viable framework for ending family homelessness; it is now up to government officials and the public to recognize it and put it to work. Simply put, if we are ever going to end family homelessness as we have known it, we have to realize that it will take a community to do so—a new community of opportunity, which begins in shelters themselves. If we don't, we will be faced with yet another generation of homeless families and children, idling in shelters across this country, waiting for the housing that may never come. For the time being at least, a shelter has indeed become a home.

NOTES

1. New York City Commission on the Homeless, *The Way Home: A New Direction in Social Policy* (New York: New York City Commission on the Homeless, 1992) 75.

2. Institute for Children and Poverty, *Together in Learning Family Literacy Curriculum* (New York: Institute for Children and Poverty, 1996). Available at: <www.instituteforchildrenandpoverty.org>.

3. National Institute for Literacy, *Frequently Asked Questions.* Available at: <http://www.nifl.gov/nifl/faqs.html#literacy%20rates>.

4. Institute for Children and Poverty, *Back to the Future: The Brownstone and FutureLink After-School Programs for Homeless Children* (New York: Institute for Children and Poverty, 2001).

5. Ibid.

6. Ibid.

7. Ralph Nunez, "Access to Success: Meeting the Educational Needs of Homeless Children," *Social Work In Education,* 1994.

8. Institute for Children and Poverty, *Job Readiness.*

9. Institute for Children and Poverty, *The Hidden Migration.*

10. Institute for Children and Poverty, *Homelessness: The Foster Care Connection* (New York: Institute for Children and Poverty, 1997).

11. Institute for Children and Poverty, *Children Having Children.*

12. Institute for Children and Poverty, *Déjà Vu;* Kenning, Merchant, and Tompkins, 238.

13. Institute for Children and Poverty, *Déjà Vu.*

14. Laura M. Caruso and Ralph da Costa Nunez, *The American Family Inn Handbook: A How-to Guide* (New York: White Tiger Press, 2002) 31.

15. Caruso, Nunez, *The American Family Inn Handbook,* 83; The Tier II Coalition.

BIBLIOGRAPHY

PUBLISHED BOOKS, ARTICLES, AND REPORTS

Bartlet, Sheridan. "The Significance of Relocation for Chronically Poor Families in the USA." *Environment and Urbanization.* Vol. 9, no. 1, 1997.

Basler, Barbara. "Koch Limits Using Welfare Hotels." *New York Times* 17 Dec. 1985.

Basler, Barbara. "Welfare Hotels Sued Over Taxes." *New York Times* 27 Dec. 1985.

Bernstein, Andrea and Amy Eddings. "Handshake Hotels: Part 1." *Morning Edition.* National Public Radio. WNYC, New York. 25 Jun. 2003.

Bernstein, Andrea and Amy Eddings. "Handshake Hotels: Part 3; How a Few Big Landlords Benefit From NYC's Homeless Placement System." *Morning Edition.* National Public Radio. WNYC, New York. 27 Jun. 2003.

Bernstein, Nina. "A Plan To End City Homelessness In Ten Years." *New York Times* 13 Jun. 2002.

Bernstein, Nina. "Homeless Shelters in NY Filled to the Highest Level Since '80s." *New York Times* 17 Jan. 2002.

Bernstein, Nina. "Many More Children Calling New York City Shelters Home." *New York Times* 13 Feb. 2001.

Bernstein, Nina. "Mentally Ill Boy Kills Himself in Shelter Hotel." *New York Times* 8 Aug. 2002.

"Bloomberg Administration Seeks More Aggressive Plan for the

Homeless." *Associated Press* 18 Jun. 2002.

Bulmiller, Elizabeth. "In Wake of Attack, Giuliani Cracks Down on Homeless." *New York Times* 20 Nov. 1999.

Burt, Martha. *Over the Edge: The Growth of Homelessness in the 1980s.* New York: Russell Sage Foundation, 1992.

Castro, Laura. "Bankers Trust Funds Housing for Homeless." *Newsday* 19 Aug. 1990.

Coalition for the Homeless. *The Right to Shelter for Homeless New Yorkers: Twenty Years and Counting.* New York: Coalition for the Homeless, 2002.

Coates, Ta-Nehisi. "Empty Promises: Housing Activists Say the City Wastes Its Vacant Lots." *The Village Voice* 12 Mar. 2003.

Cooper, Michael. "Jail Reopens as a Shelter for Families." *New York Times* 12 Aug. 2002.

"Cuomo Makes Visit to Homeless." *New York Times* 19 Dec. 1985.

Daskal, Jennifer. *In Search of Shelter: The Growing Shortage of Affordable Housing Units.* Washington, DC: Center for Budget and Policy Priorities, 1988.

Egan, Jennifer. "To Be Young and Homeless." *New York Times Magazine* 24 Mar. 2002.

Goodwin, Michael. "Carol Bellamy Fights Sharing of Apartments of Homeless Families." *New York Times* 28 Jun. 1984.

Goodwin, Michael. "State is Penalizing City Over Shelter Conditions." *New York Times* 21 Dec. 1983.

Grossman, Jill. "Shelter Skelter." *City Limits Magazine.* Mar. 2002.

Hemphill, Clara. "The High Price of Sheltering City's Homeless." *Newsday* 2 Dec. 1988.

Herbert, Bob. "In America; Children in Crisis." *New York Times* 10 Jun. 1999.

Hewlett, S.A. *When the Bough Breaks: The Cost of Neglecting Our Children.* New York: Basic Books, 1991.

Heyback, Laurene M. and Patricia Nix-Hodes. "Reducing Mobility: Good for Kids, Good for Schools." *The Beam: The Newsletter of the National Association for the Education of Homeless Children and Youth.* vol. 9, no. 1, 1999.

"Homelessness Emerges as Campaign Issue for Clinton and Giuliani." *CNN.* 5 Dec. 1999. Available at: <http://www.cnn.com>

Institute for Children and Poverty. *A Tale of Two Cities: Family Homelessness in Connecticut.* New York: Institute for Children and Poverty, 2003.

Institute for Children and Poverty. *Children Having Children: Teen Pregnancy and Homelessness in New York City.* New York: Institute for Children and Poverty, 2003.

Institute for Children and Poverty. *Miles to Go: The Flip Side of the McKinney-Vento Homeless Assistance Act.* New York: Institute for Children and Poverty, 2003.

Institute for Children and Poverty. *Hidden Migration: Why New York City Shelters Are Overflowing with Families.* New York: Institute for Children and Poverty, 2002.

Institute for Children and Poverty. *Back to the Future: The Brownstone and FutureLink After-School Programs for Homeless Children.* New York: Institute for Children and Poverty, 2002.

Institute for Children and Poverty. *What New Jersey Needs to Know. . . About Family Homelessness.* New York: Institute for Children and Poverty, 2002.

Institute for Children and Poverty. *A Shelter is Not a Home—Or is it?* New York: Institute for Children and Poverty, 2001.

Institute for Children and Poverty. *Déjà Vu: Family Homelessness in New York City.* New York: Institute for Children and Poverty, 2001.

Institute for Children and Poverty. *The Other America: Homeless Families in the Shadow of a New Economy—Family Homelessness in Kentucky, Tennessee and the Carolinas.* New

York: Institute for Children and Poverty, 2000.

Institute for Children and Poverty. *Multiple Families: Multiplying Problems: A First Look at the Fathers of Homeless Children.* New York: Institute for Children and Poverty, 2000.

Institute for Children and Poverty. *Homeless In America: A Children's Story.* New York: Institute for Children and Poverty, 1999.

Institute for Children and Poverty. A Welfare Reform-Homelessness-Foster Care Connection?; The Story of "Lag Families" and "Limbo Children" in San Diego. New York: Institute for Children and Poverty, 1999.

Institute for Children and Poverty. *Inside the Beltway: The State of Homeless Children in Washington, D.C.* New York: Institute for Children and Poverty, 1999.

Institute for Children and Poverty. *Ten Cities: A Snapshot of Family Homelessness Across America, 1997-1998.* New York: Institute for Children and Poverty, 1998.

Institute for Children and Poverty. *Up the Down Staircase: A Look at Family Homelessness in New Jersey.* New York: Institute for Children and Poverty, 1998.

Institute for Children and Poverty. *A Trail of Tears. . . Trapped in a Cycle of Violence and Homelessness.* Institute for Children and Poverty, 1998.

Institute for Children and Poverty. *Day to Day. . . Parent to Child: The Future of Violence Among Homeless Children in America.* New York: Institute for Children and Poverty, 1998.

Institute for Children and Poverty. *Homeless Families Today: Our Challenge Tomorrow.* New York: Institute for Children and Poverty, 1998.

Institute for Children and Poverty. *The Cycle of Homelessness: A Social Policy Reader.* New York: Institute for Children and Poverty, 1998.

Institute for Children and Poverty. *Common Sense: Why Jobs and*

Training Alone Won't End Welfare for Homeless Families in America. New York: Institute for Children and Poverty, 1997.

Institute for Children and Poverty. *Homelessness: The Foster Care Connection.* New York: Institute for Children and Poverty, 1997.

Institute for Children and Poverty. *The Dollars and Sense of Welfare: Why Work Alone Won't Work.* New York: Institute for Children and Poverty, 1996.

Institute for Children and Poverty. *The Age of Confusion: Why So Many Teens are Getting Pregnant, Turning to Welfare, and Ending Up Homeless.* New York: Institute for Children and Poverty, 1996.

Institute for Children and Poverty. *A Tale of Two Nations: The Creation of "Poverty Nomads."* New York: Institute for Children and Poverty, 1996.

Institute for Children and Poverty. *An American Family Myth: Every Child at Risk.* New York: Institute for Children and Poverty, 1995.

Institute for Children and Poverty. *Job Readiness: Crossing the Threshold from Homelessness to Employment.* New York: Institute for Children and Poverty, 1994.

Institute for Children and Poverty. *Access to Success: Meeting the Educational Needs of Homeless Children.* New York: Institute for Children and Poverty, 1993.

Institute for Children and Poverty. *The New Poverty: A Generation of Homeless Families.* New York: Institute for Children and Poverty, 1992.

Kaufman, Leslie. "Manhattan: No Cruise Ships for Homeless." *The New York Times* 18 Jun. 2003.

Kenning, M., A. Merchant, and A. Tomkins. "Research on the Effects of Witnessing Parental Battering: Clinical and Legal Policy Implications." *Women Battering: Policy Responses.* Cincinnatti, OH: Anderson, 1991.

Kozol, Jonathan. *Rachel and Her Children.* New York: Crown, 1988.

Kusmer, Kenneth. *Down And Out and On the Road: The Homeless in American History.* New York: Oxford University Press, 2002.

Leonard, Paul, Cushing N. Dolbeare, and Edward B. Lazare. *A Place to Call Home: The Crisis in Housing for the Poor.* Washington, D.C.: Center for Budget and Policy Priorities, 1989.

Lueck, Thomas. "Breaking Ground in Housing Policy." *New York Times* 30 Apr. 1989.

McMillan, Tracie. "Sleep Disorder." *City Limits* 4 Jan. 2002.

Mishel, L., J Bernstein and J. Schmitt. *The State of Working America: 1998-1999.* Washington, D.C.: Economic Policy Institute, 1999.

Mihaly, L.K. *Homeless Families: Failed Policies and Young Victims.* Washington, D.C.: The Children's Defense Fund, 1991.

National Jobs With Peace Campaign. *Fact Sheet.* Boston, 1990.

National Low Income Housing Coalition. *Changing Priorities: The Federal Budget and Housing Assistance 1976-2007.* Washington, D.C.: National Low Income Housing Coalition, 1990.

"New York Barred from Placing Needy Families in Midtown Hotels." *Associated Press* 21 Dec. 1986.

Nix, Crystal. "Housing Family in a Shelter Costs the City $70,000 Per Year." *New York Times* 7 Mar. 1986.

Nix, Crystal. "Profits of Welfare Hotels Placed at $3M." *New York Times* 23 Nov. 1985.

Nunez, Ralph and Laura M. Caruso. *The American Family Inn Handbook: A How-to Guide.* New York: White Tiger Press, 2002.

Nunez, Ralph. "Family Homelessness in New York City: A Case Study." *Political Science Quarterly* 113 (Fall 2001): 367-379.

Nunez, Ralph. "Breaking the Cycle: Educating America's Homeless Children." In *By Design and Neglect, The Education of Homeless and Street Children in the United States and Brazil.* Edited by J. Anyon and R.A. Mickelson. 2000.

Nunez, Ralph and C. Fox. "A Snapshot of Family Homelessness Across America." *Political Science Quarterly* 114, no. 2 (Summer 1999): 289-307.

Nunez, Ralph and K. Collignon. "Creating a Community of Learning for Homeless Children." In *Educational Leadership* 55, no. 2 (October 1997): 56-60.

Nunez, Ralph. "The Homeless in the New Era of Welfare Reform: A View from the Trenches." *Metropolitics* 1, no. 3 (Winter 1997): 14-16.

Nunez, Ralph. "Shelters Can Help the Homeless." In *The Homeless.* Edited by T.L. Roleff. San Diego, CA: Greenhaven Press, Inc.

Nunez, Ralph. *The New Poverty; Homeless Families in America.* New York: Insight Books, 1996.

Nunez, Ralph. "Family Values Among Homeless Families." *Public Welfare* 53, no. 4 (Fall 1995): 24-32.

Nunez, Ralph. "Access to Success: Meeting the Educational Needs of Homeless Children." *Social Work In Education,* 1994.

Nunez, Ralph. *Hopes, Dreams, and Promise: The Future of Homeless Children in America.* New York: Homes for the Homeless, 1994.

Nunez, Ralph. "The New Poverty: A Generation of Homeless Families." *American College Journal of Business* (Spring, 1993).

"NYC's Homeless Lockjam." Editorial. *New York Times* 14 Aug. 2002.

Olsson, Elizabeth. "A Real Estate Bargain; A Push for Expanding Supportive Housing to Stem a Growing Homeless Crisis." *City Limits* Jul./Aug. 2002.

Rafferty, Yvonne and Norma Rollins. *Learning in Limbo: The*

Educational Deprivation of Young Homeless Children. New York: Advocates for Children of New York, Inc., 1989.

Redlener, Irwin. *Still In Crisis: The Health Status of New York's Homeless Children.* New York: Children's Defense Fund, 1999.

Reich, R.B. "As the World Turns." *New Republic* (3876) 1989.

Rosenman, Mark and Mary Lee Stein. "Homeless Children: A New Vulnerability." *Homeless Children: The Watchers and Waiters.* Binghamton: Haworth Press, 1990.

Sandel, Meagan, Joshua Sharfstein, and Randy Shaw. *There's No Place Like Home: How America's Housing Crisis Threatens Our Children.* San Francisco: Housing America, 1999.

Second Harvest, *Who We Serve/Hunger: The Faces & Facts, Health and Social Consequences.* Chicago: Second Harvest, 1999.

Steinhauer, Jennifer. "A Jail Becomes a Shelter, and Maybe a Mayor's Albatross." *New York Times* 13 Aug. 2002.

The Joint Center for Housing Studies. *The State of the Nation's Housing: 2000,* Cambridge: Harvard University 2000.

Topousis, Tom. "Shellacked by Slumlords." *New York Post* 19 May 2003.

Topousis, Tom. "They Owe, We Pay." *New York Post* 19 May 2003.

Torrey, E. Fuller. "Stop the Madness." *Wall Street Journal* 18 Jul. 1997.

Wilgoren, Jody. "After Welfare, Working Poor Still Struggle, Report Finds." *New York Times* 25 Apr. 2002.

Zucchino, David. *The Myth of the Welfare Queen.* New York: Touchstone, Simon and Schuster, 1997.

GOVERNMENT DOCUMENTS AND REPORTS

Independent Budget Office. *Inside the Budget.* New York: Independent Budget Office, 12 Sept. 2002.

Manhattan Borough President's Task Force on Housing and Homeless Families. *A Shelter Is Not A Home.* New York:

Manhattan Borough President's Task Force on Housing for Homeless Families, 1987.

Mayor's Press Office. "Mayor Giuliani Opens Coney Island Job Center." *Press Release #239-01*, 5 Jul. 2001.

New York City Commission on the Homeless. *The Way Home: A New Direction in Social Policy.* New York: New York City Commission on the Homeless, 1992.

New York City Department of Homeless Services, Office of Policy and Planning. *Critical Activities Report, Family Services- Fiscal Year 2003.* New York: Department of Homeless Services, 2003.

New York City Department of Homeless Services. *Critical Activities Report- Fiscal Year 2003.* New York: New York City Department of Homeless Services, Jan. 2003.

New York City Department of Homeless Services. *Implementing a New Vision for the Next Decade.* New York: New York City Department of Homeless Services, 2003.

New York City Department of Homeless Services. *Reforming New York City's System of Homeless Services.* New York: New York City Department of Homeless Services, 1994.

New York City Department of Homeless Services. *The Second Decade of Reform: A Strategic Plan for New York City's Homeless Services.* New York: New York City Department of Homeless Services, 2002.

New York City Department of Housing Preservation and Development. *HPD Announces New Round of Building Blocks!* Available at: <http://www.nyc.gov./html/hpd/html/archive/rfq1-pr.html>.

New York City Department of Housing Preservation and Development. *2002 Housing and Vacancy Survey: Initial Findings.* New York: New York City Department of Housing Preservation and Development, 2002.

New York City Department of Housing, Preservation, and

Development. *1999 Housing and Vacancy Survey: Initial Findings.* New York: New York City Department of Housing Preservation and Development, 1999.

New York City Human Resources Administration. *Mayor's Management Report.* New York: New York City Human Resources Administration, 1983.

New York City Human Resources Administration. *Mayor's Management Report.* New York: New York City Human Resources Administration, 1985.

New York City Human Resources Administration. *Mayor's Management Report.* New York: New York City Human Resources Administration, 1986.

New York City Human Resources Administration. *Mayor's Management Report.* New York: New York City Human Resources Administration, 1988.

New York City Human Resources Administration. *Mayor's Management Report.* New York: New York City Human Resources Administration, 1993.

New York City Human Resources Administration. *Mayor's Management Report.* New York: New York City Human Resources Administration, 1994.

New York City Human Resources Administration. *Mayor's Management Report.* New York: New York City Human Resources Administration, 1995.

New York City Human Resources Administration. *Mayor's Management Report.* New York: New York City Human Resources Administration, 1996.

New York City Human Resources Administration. *Mayor's Management Report.* New York: New York City Human Resources Administration, 1997.

New York City Human Resources Administration. *Mayor's Management Report.* New York: New York City Human Resources Administration, 1998.

New York City Human Resources Administration. *Mayor's Management Report.* New York: New York City Human Resources Administration, 1999.

New York City Human Resources Administration. *Mayor's Management Report Preliminary Fiscal.* New York: New York City Human Resources Administration, 2003.

New York City Human Resources Administration. *Running Out of Time: The Impact of Federal Welfare Reform.* New York: New York City Human Resources Administration, 2001.

New York State Department of Family Assistance. *Domestic Violence: Frequently Asked Questions on Reimbursement, General and Programmatic Issues.* New York: New York State Department of Family Assistance, 30 Sept. 2002.

Stegman, Michael. *Housing and Vacancy Report: New York City.* New York: Department of Housing Preservation and Development, 1987.

U.S. Census Bureau. *Poverty.* 2002. Availabe at: <http://www.census.gov/population/www/pop-profile/poverty.html>.

U.S. Department of Housing and Urban Development. *Martinez, Pataki and Bloomberg Announce $50 Million Affordable Housing Initiative in Lower Manhattan.* New York: U.S. Department of Housing and Urban Development, 2003. Available at: <http://www.hud.gov/news>.

U.S. Department of Housing and Urban Development. *Waiting In Vain: An Update on America's Housing Crisis.* Washington, D.C.: U.S. Department of Housing and Urban Development, 1999.

UNPUBLISHED SOURCES

The New York City Department of Homeless Services. *About the Department.* Available at:
    <http://www.nyc.gov/html/dhs/html/aboutnycdhs.html>.

NYC Rental Guidelines Board. *Affordable Housing: Where Can*

You Find the Lowest Rents? Available at: <http://www.housingnyc.com/guide/location/html>.

Gibbs, Linda. "City Council Testimony." New York City Council Meeting. City Hall, New York. 18 Sept. 2002.

Children's Aid Society. *History.* Available at: <http://www.childrensaidsociety.org/about/history>.

New York City Human Resources Administration. *HRA Facts: January 2003.* Available at: <http://www.nyc.gov/html/hra/html.hrafacts.html/>.

Institute for Children and Poverty. *Unpublished Data.* Aug. 2003.

The Annie E. Casey Foundation. *Kids Count.* Available at: <http://www.aecf.org>.

Murphy, Ken. Personal interview. 26 Feb. 2002.

National Bureau of Economic Research, Bureau of Labor Statistics; New York State Department of Labor, 1992.

Coalition for the Homeless. *New York Kids Need Housing!* Available at: <http://www.coalitionforthehomeless.org>.

Coalition for the Homeless. *Preserve the Right to Shelter: History.* Available at: <http://www.right2shelter.org/history.htm>.

Schatt, Larry. Personal interview. 8 Feb. 2002.

United Neighborhood Houses. *Settlement House History.* Available at: <http://www.unhny.org/about/settlement.cfm>.

Housing First! *The Housing New York Ten Year Plan.* Available at: <http://www.housingfirst.net/policypaper_app_b.html>.

Tuchelli, Sal. Personal interview. 12 Apr. 2002.

Wackstein, Nancy. Personal interview. 15 Mar. 2002.

PHOTOGRAPHY CREDITS

All photos by David Nevala, James Farnum, Todd Flashner, Mathew Septimus, Erin Thompson, or Jesse Ellison used with the permission of Homes for the Homeless, with the exception of:

PHOTO INSERT:

Page 1:   Bottom right: © Mark Peterson/Corbis.
Page 2:   Bottom: © Mark Peterson/Corbis.
Page 3:   Bottom: © Bob Rowan; Progressive Image/ Corbis.
Page 5:   Top: © Mike Zens/Corbis
Page 6:   Bottom: © Mark Peterson/Corbis

INDEX

Acquired Immune Deficiency Syndrome (AIDS), 12
Affordable housing. See Low-income housing
Aid to Families with Dependent Children (AFDC)
Clinton administration, 44
cuts in, 10
origin of, 3–4
public opinion, 14–15
Asthma, 96–97

Birth control, knowledge of, 82
Bloomberg, Michael, 52, 55, 56, 57, 62
Bronx House of Detention, 56
Building Blocks! initiative, 48–49

Callahan v. Carey, 15
Callahan decree (1981), 50
Carter Hotel, 22
Child abuse, homeless parents, 79
Child custody. See also Foster care system
shelter system, 57
work requirements, 50
Children. See Homeless children
Children's Aid Society, 2
Civilian Conservation Corps (CCC), 3
Clinton, Hillary Rodham, 50
Clinton, William J., 44, 45, 113
Clinton Family Inn, xix
Commission on Homelessness (NYC), 31
Communities of opportunity, 103–115. See also Shelter system; Tier II facilities
community interactions, 110–114
domestic violence, 109–110
education, 105–107
employment, 107–108
foster care, 108–109

health, 110
teenage pregnancy, 109
Congregate placements. See
    Tier I facilities
Costs. See also Economic fac-
    tors
    communities of opportuni-
        ty, 111
    foster care, 108
    McKinney Homeless
        Assistance Act of 1987,
        37–38
    rental vouchers, EARP, 35
    scattered site housing,
        60–61
    shelter system, 24–25, 59
    supportive housing, 69–70
    Tier I facilities, 21, 32
    Tier II facilities, 32, 61
    welfare hotels, 21–22, 23,
        24, 60
Court challenges
    Emergency Assistance
        Units, 47, 56
    homelessness, 15, 19, 32,
        34
    "special master panel," 57
    Tier II facilities, 50
Crack cocaine epidemic, 7, 12
Crime
    growth in early 1980s, 7
    Guiliani administration, 43,
        51

homelessness, 50, 51
    welfare hotels, 22
Crisis nurseries, 108
Cruise ships, 60
Cuomo, Andrew, 113
Custody. See Child custody

De-institutionalization, of
    mental patients, 4
"Demonstration Project," 57
Department of Homeless
    Services (DHS, NYC),
    29, 31, 46, 47, 60,
    61–62
Department of Housing and
    Urban Development
    (HUD). See U.S.
    Department of Housing
    and Urban Development
    (HUD)
Department of Housing
    Preservation and
    Development (HPD,
    NYC), 25, 32, 48
Deserving poor, undeserving
    poor and, 3
Dinkins, David, 29, 30, 31,
    35–36
Domestic violence
    communities of opportu-
        nity, 109–110
    effects of, 77–78
    foster care system, 79

Drake, Paris, 50
Dropouts, 95
Drug abuse
   poverty, 12
   welfare hotels, 22

Economic factors. *See also*
      Costs
   income requirements, low-
      income housing, 104
   income statistics, New York
      City, 67
   minimum wage, 1980s, 9
   recession of early 1980s,
      8–9
   recession of early 1990s,
      43–44
   recession of 2000 to pres-
      ent, 86
Education
   communities of opportuni-
      ty, 105–107
   homeless children, 91–92
   job readiness, 83–84
Eldrege v. Koch, 15
Emergency Assistance
      Rehousing Program
      (EARP), 34–37, 69
Emergency Assistance Units
      (EAU)
   application process in, 59,
      75–76
   closure of, threatened,

46–47
   crowding in, 29, 56
   domestic violence, 78
   role of, 19–20
Emergency shelter system. *See*
      Shelter system
Emotional well-being, home
      less children, 98–99
Employment. *See*
      Unemployment
Environmental Control Board
      (NYC), 22
Evictions, Department of
      Homeless Services (DHS,
      NYC), 62

Families, in shelters, xvii, 7–8,
      52. *See also* Homeless
      children; Homelessness;
      Homeless parents; Shelter
      system
Family Assistance and Safety
      Net Assistance Program
      (NYS), 45
Family Assistance (FA), limits
      on, 85
Family centers approach, 26
Federal government
   Great Depression, 3
   homeless parents, 84–86
   housing assistance by,
      37–38
   housing assistance cuts by,

10–12, 49, 66, 113
social service cuts by, 9–10,
   113–114
Federal Transient Program
   (FTP), 3
Feerick, John D., 57
Food stamps
   cuts in, 10
   origin of, 4
Foster care system. See also
   Child custody
   communities of opportun-
      ity, 108–109
   homeless parents, 78–81
   welfare reductions, 86
Fraud, Emergency Assistance
   Units, 20

Giuliani, Rudolph, 38–39, 43,
   44, 45, 46, 47–48, 50,
   51–52, 56, 59, 60
Great Depression, 3

Hamilton Hotel, 60
Harrington, Michael, 4
Head Start, 4
Health
   communities of opportun-
      ity, 110
   homeless children, 96–97
Helmsley, Harry, 7
Hogue, Larry, 50
Holland Hotel, 22, 23

Homeless children, 91–102.
   See also Homelessness;
   Homeless parents; Shelter
   system
   AFDC program, 14–15
   custody of, 50, 57
   education, 91–92, 105–107
   emotional well-being,
      98–99
   health, 96–97, 110
   historical perspective, 2
   hunger, 97–98
   interactions among factors,
      99
   parent education, 96
   preschool programs, 95
   recommendations for,
      99–100
   school system, 92–95
   in shelter system, xviii–xix,
      1, 7–8, 52, 91
Homelessness. See also
   Homeless children;
   Homeless parents;
   Shelter system
   children, xviii–xix, 1, 7–8,
      14–15
   court challenges, 15, 19, 32
   families, xvii
   growth in, 7–8
   Guiliani administration,
      38–39, 46
   historical perspective, 2–5

increases in, 55
public opinion, 14, 38,
    49–51
recidivism rates, 32, 103
roots of, xxi–xxii, 12–13, 71
term of, 14
Homeless parents, 75–89. See
    also Homeless children;
    Homelessness; Shelter sy-
    stem
domestic violence, 77–78
education of, 96
foster care system, 78–81
historical perspective, 75
job readiness, 82–84
parent-child literacy pro-
    grams, 105
profile of, 75–77
racial profile of, 76
recommendations for,
    86–87
teenage pregnancy, 81–82
welfare reform, 84–86
Homeless Persons' Survival
    Act, 37
Homes for the Homeless,
    founding and growth of,
    xviii, xix–xx
Hotels. See Welfare hotels
Housing, historical perspective,
    2. See also Low-income
    housing; Public housing
Housing assistance, cuts in,

10–12. See also Low-
    income housing; Public
    housing
Housing Authority. See New
    York City Housing
    Authority (NYCHA)
Housing New York plan, 25
Human Resources
    Administration (NYC),
    24, 31, 32–33, 46–47,
    78
Hunger, homeless children,
    97–98

Immigration, 2
Income Maintenance Centers
    (IMs), 19
Income requirements, low-
    income housing, 104
Income statistics, New York
    City, 67
Income Support Center, 47
In rem buildings, 25, 48
Institute for Children and
    Poverty, xx

Job Centers (NYC), 45–46
Job readiness, homeless parents,
    82–84
Johnson, Lyndon B., 4

Kean, Thomas H., 13
Koch, Edward, xvii, 2, 25, 29,

30, 31, 35
Kronenfeld, Daniel, 57

Legal Aid Society, 15, 57, 62
Literacy programs, parent-
 child, 105
Low-income housing
 decline in, 10–12, 58,
  65–66, 113
 Guiliani administration,
  47–48
 income requirements for,
  104
 New York City, 66–68
 in rem buildings, 25, 48
 solutions for, 68–71

Martinique Hotel, 22
McCain v. Koch, 15, 20, 32
McKinney, Stewart B., 37
McKinney Federal Homeless
 Assistance Act of 1987,
 37–38, 92, 93
Media
 domestic violence, 78
 homelessness, 14, 50, 61
 welfare hotels, 22–24
Medicaid, 4
Mental patients
 de-institutionalization of, 4
 homelessness, 49–50, 51
Minimum wage, 1980s, 9
Morton, James Parks, xvii–xviii

Nayowirth, Gail B., 57
New Deal, 3
New York City Department of
 Homeless Services (DHS,
 NYC), 29, 31, 46, 47, 60,
 61–62
New York City Department of
 Housing Preservation and
 Development (HPD,
 NYC), 25, 32, 48
New York City Housing
 Authority (NYCHA),
 36–37
New York State
 Safety Net Assistance
  Program (NYS), 45
 Tier I facilities, 20
Non-profit sector, Tier II facili
 ties, 32–33, 50
Not-in-my-backyard (NIMBY)
 attitude, Tier II facilities,
 33–34
Nurseries, 108
Nutrition, homeless children,
 97–98

Omnibus Budget
 Reconciliation Act of
 1981, 10

Parent-child literacy programs,
 105

Parents. See Homeless parents
Pataki, George, 50
Personal Responsibility and
    Work Opportunity Act of
    1996, 44, 84–85
Philanthropic organizations,
    historical perspective, 2–3
Poverty. See also Homeless chil
    dren; Homelessness;
    Homeless parents
    deserving poor/undeserving
    poor dichotomy, 3
    Giuliani administration, 51
    growth in early 1980s, 7, 9
    public opinion, 14–15
Preschool programs, homeless
    children, 95
Prospect Family Inn, xviii
Public assistance
    growth in early 1980s, 7
    mid 1990s statistics, 44–45,
    49
Public housing. See also Low-
    income housing
    abandonment of, 66, 113
    wait lists for, 20, 36–37, 66
Public opinion
    homelessness, 14, 38, 49–51
    Tier II facilities, 33–34
    welfare hotels, 24

"Quality of life" campaign,
    Guiliani administration,
43

Racial profile, homeless fami-
    lies, 76
Reagan, Ronald, 9, 10–11, 37,
    66, 113
Recession
    of 2000, 86
    homeless parents, 86
    of 1980s, 8–9
    of 1990s, 43–44
Recidivism rates, homeless-
    ness, 32, 103
Rental subsidies and vouchers
    EARP, 35
    expansion of, 57–58
    low-income housing, 68–69
Rents
    increases in, 11–12
    New York City, 66–68
Retired cruise ships, 60
Riis, Jacob, 2
Roberto Clemente family shel-
    ter, xvii, 14, 20
Roosevelt, Franklin D., 3

Safety Net Assistance Program
    (NYS), 45
Saratoga Family Inn, xviii, xix,
    94
Scattered site housing, growth
    in, 60–62
School dropouts, 95

School system, homeless chil
 dren, 92–95
Shelter system. See also
 Communities of opportu-
 nity; Homelessness
 budget of, 16
 child custody, 57
 costs of, 24–25, 59
 domestic violence, 78
 early 1980s, 7–18
 future prospects, 103–104
 growth in, 7–8, 29
 Guiliani administration,
 38–39
 late 1990s and after, 55–64
 late 1980s and early 1990s,
 29–41
 mid 1980s, 19–28, 103
 mid 1990s, 43–53
Social Security Act of 1936,
 3–4
Social service cuts, federal government, 9–10
Special Initiatives Program
 (SIP), 25, 35, 36
"Special master panel," estab-
 lishment of, 57
Springfield Family Inn, xix
Squatters, removal of, 48
Subsidized housing. See Low-
 income housing; Public
 housing; Rental subsidies
Suicide, 56

Summer camps, xix–xx
Supportive housing, low-
 income housing, 69–70

Teenage pregnancy
 communities of opportun-
 ity, 109
 homeless parents, 81–82
Temporary Assistance for
 Needy Families (TANF),
 44–45
Ten-Year Plan, 113–114
Tier I facilities
 courts and, 32
 role of, 20–21
Tier II facilities. See also
 Communities of opportu-
 nity
 community interactions,
 111–114
 community resistance to,
 33–34
 costs of, 61
 Emergency Assistance
 Rehousing Program
 (EARP), 34–37
 Giuliani administration, 50
 move toward, 30, 31–33
 origin of, 26
 placement process, 58, 59
 supportive housing, 69
"Together In Learning" program, 105

Training programs, job readiness, 84. *See also*
Education
Transitional housing, move towards, 26
Trump, Donald, 7

Undeserving poor, deserving poor and, 3
Unemployment
communities of opportunity, 107–108
job readiness, 82–84
recession of early 1980s, 8–9
recession of early 1990s, 43–44
recession of 2000 to present, 86
U.S. Department of Education, 95
U.S. Department of Housing and Urban Development (HUD), 11, 49, 58
Urbanization, 2

Vacancy rates, New York City, 67
Vietnam War, 4
Violence. *See* Domestic violence
Vouchers. *See* Rental subsidies and vouchers

War on Poverty, 4
Welfare. *See* Aid to Families with Dependent Children (AFDC); Public assistance
Welfare hotels, 5, 13
Bloomberg administration, 60, 61
courts and, 32
Dinkins administration, 30
media and, 22–24
role of, 21–22
Work Experience Program (WEP, NYC), 45, 46, 85
Work requirements
historical perspective, 3
homeless parents, 85–86
shelter system, 50
Temporary Assistance for Needy Familics (TANF), 44–45
Works Project Administration (WPA), 3
World Trade Center attack, 51, 55